Introduction

Left: The ultimate expression in very heavy bombing. The B-29 was a huge step in technology yet came with more than its fair share of challenges. (USAF)

Below: The B-17 allowed Boeing to understand the complexities of mass large aircraft construction, paving the way for B-29 construction. (Library of Congress)

The Boeing B-29 Superfortress, named in reference to its smaller predecessor, the B-17, was the definitive expression in piston-powered offensive and strategic air power. It was designed for an air force that was slowly realising it needed larger and heavier aircraft to undertake missions thousands of miles away from its home bases. The B-29 was riding on the wave of the equally ground-breaking Boeing B-17, with Boeing using this experience, both in terms of manufacturing and user feedback, to create a bigger, more capable and more complex platform. The B-29 would go on to incorporate all the lessons learned from the European and early Pacific air wars in its design and subsequent operational handling. It would also fulfil the role of next-generation, increasingly sophisticated aircraft for an organisation still adapting to using its heavy bombers – the B-17 and Consolidated B-24 – effectively.

The story of the B-29 is also unique in that it was an aeroplane which was placed into production before the usual prototype shakedowns. Where the B-17 had over thirty month's development between first flight and operational use, the B-29 had none. The need for this aeroplane, and more importantly its load-carrying capabilities, allied to the urgency to win the war against Imperial Japan, led to a Herculean effort by all to straighten out issues as they occurred.

The B-29 was a genuine behemoth of the skies and its flight endurance would see its ten-man crew supplied with rest bunks, remotely operated defensive guns and a tunnel linking the front and rear of the aircraft. It was also tough, capable of using

A crowd attends the delivery ceremony of the 1,000th B-29 at Boeing-Wichita, Kansas, on 14 February 1945. (NARA)

B-29s at Boeing-Wichita plant await the final manufacturer's tests. (NARA)

Pride in a job well done. Boeing's manufacturer's plaque on B-29 'Doc', one of two B-29s still flying. (Tech. Sergeant Alexander Riede/USAF)

the most basic landing strips, provided they were long enough.

Completed aircraft came straight from the factory floors and immediately into retro-fitting as snags were identified. The B-29 was, to all intents and purposes, a huge commercial, military and political gamble. The men and women who worked in often-appalling conditions to ensure the United States Army Air Force (USAAF) had their new Very Heavy Bomber (VHB) were the key to the success of the B-29.

The B-29's exceptional range of 3,250 miles (5,230km) would find its natural home in the Pacific Theatre. Once the numerous issues, from logistics to crew training, were addressed, its payload would go on to wreak havoc among the forces of Imperial Japan. As well as military targets, the B-29s grouped together in the specially formed 20th Air Force (AF), would strike hard against targets in occupied areas as well as the Japanese Home Islands.

The 20th AF would fly its B-29s from bases established in India and China from June 1944 before following behind MacArthur's island-hopping push towards the Japanese Home Islands. The 20th would establish new bases among the liberated Mariana islands which would place them ever closer to their targets. It was from one of these islands, Tinian, that B-29s would take off with the nuclear weapons that would be dropped on the cities of Hiroshima and Nagasaki.

The B-29 has more than earned its place in the halls of aviation fame. It was an aircraft ahead of its time that helped usher in a new age of military aviation and provideed a tangible bridge between new and old ways.

In the post-war era the B-29 was retained by the USAAF, and from 1948 by the USAF, as the primary strategic bomber. However, the B-29's fighting days were far from over;,it would go on to see action over the skies of Korea and would supplement the Royal Air Force's (RAF) bomber capacity while Bomber Command awaited the arrival of the Canberra and its next generation jet-powered V-bombers.

The B-29 would unwittingly also help kick start the long-range heavy-bomber programmes of the USSR, as reverse-engineered interned examples, and go on to produce the Tupolev Tu-4. This would also be used by the Chinese People's Liberation Army Air Force (PLAAF), who maintained the type in service until 1988, some twenty-eight years after the B-29, the B-50 with its engine upgrade, and the Tu-4, had been retired by the USAF and USSR.

Picture showing the devastation caused by the bomb dropped on Hiroshima on 6 August 1945. (Hiroshima Museum)

General Joseph 'Vinegar Joe' Stilwell in conference with Major General Curtis LeMay, commander of the XX Bomber Command at a Chinese airfield, 11 October 1944. (Library of Congress)

When is a B-29 not a B-29? When it's a Tu-4 Bull. (Dmitry Avdeev)

A B-29 of the 307th Bomb Group bombing a target during the Korean War. (USAF)

Design & Development

The XB-15, seen here with a Boeing P-26 Peashooter, was not only a huge aircraft but also a huge step forward in aeronautical development. (Charles Daniels Photo Collection/ San Diego Air & Space Museum)

The father of American strategic air power, General Billy Mitchell, with a Vought VE 7 at Bolling Field Air Tournament, 14 May 1920. (USAF)

For an aircraft of its size and relative complexity the B-29 hit the ground running. It owed much of its design and development to the innovations and research previously carried out by Boeing with their XB-15 (Boeing 294). The XB-15 was an aircraft that had originally been developed for the B-17 programme, but was placed to one side because it lacked a suitable engine.

The genesis of the B-29 lay in General Billy Mitchell's advocacy of strategic air power to the American military and government. Mitchell's vision of air power was shaped by his experiences and observations during the First World War. His views of investing in air power went against the grain of contemporary US military thinking, even more so when he demonstrated the power of the aircraft against shipping in 1921, much to the United States Navy's (USN) chagrin. Mitchell's obstreperous behaviour culminated in 1925 when he accused military chiefs of 'almost treasonable administration of the national defence'; The USN had invested in more ships. This outburst led to the well-publicized court martial of Mitchell for insubordination and ultimately resulted in his resignation.

By the early 1930s there was a shift in the United States Army Air Crops' (USAAC) view of strategic air power. This was driven by the first generation of pilots who were now being promoted to field officer command positions and were able to start shaping the service using field experience. Although initially meeting resistance from General Staff, the resistance slowly waned as older commanders retired. The younger officers remained in thrall of Billy Mitchell's ideas, and aeronautical technology was catching up, capable of delivering Mitchell's dream of a bomber with a 5,000-mile (8,047km) range and 35,000ft (10,668m) ceiling. This new generation of air corps officers were soon leading departments that mattered including the Material Command based at Wright Field, Ohio. It was here that Project A was devised in July 1933, calling for a bomber capable of flying 5,000 miles with a ton of bombs.

The following April, Army General Staff approved the project based on a project outline developed by the younger officers over the previous winter. An interesting use of language had crept in and the new aircraft was deemed a hemisphere-defence aircraft and not an offensive bomber. The wording was deliberate as it actually considered political changes that were occurring in Eurasia and reflected the public mood regarding offensive weaponry. The new aircraft had to be capable of defending American interests and territories in the western hemisphere, from Alaska to Panama, and Hawaii to Puerto Rico.

Yet there remained obstacles. Mitchell's efforts had proved many things, including the USN's ability to be wary of long-range air power almost a decade later. The US War Department was lobbied by the USN to ensure any aircraft that was built under of Project A would be excluded from carrying out any maritime tasks. The USN continued to insist that it was the sole defender of continental United States from maritime threats; the consensus was, despite Mitchell proving otherwise in 1921, that military vessels were immune to air attack.

Despite USN resistance, Project A progressed and General Henry Pratt issued requests from the domestic aviation industry to meet the specifications laid

Design & Development 5

An early B-17D at Wright Field. It was here that the army air corps began to shape the strategic doctrine that would lead to the B-29's development based on experience flying the B-17. (USAF)

out by the project. On 12 May 1934 the Glenn Martin Company and Boeing Aircraft Company were selected to develop preliminary designs with the USAAC's Material Command. On 14 May the two presidents of the companies, C.A. van Dusen from Glenn Martin and Clairemont Egtvedt were invited for a briefing which ended with both companies being given a month to deliver their designs.

They returned with the Boeing Model 294 and the Glenn Martin Model 145. The Boeing design was selected, which developed into the XB-15 and started Boeing's long relationship with heavy bombers. On 15 October 1937 the four-engine XB-15 made its maiden voyage featuring a host of technical and design innovations, including a wing-crawl way to allow engineer access in flight. The XB-15 also proved that the 5,000-mile (8,047km) range was possible and gave the USAAC its first real taste of what a future heavy bomber would look like.

On the back of the work being done on the Model 294, Egtvedt ordered a side project, Model 299, which would eventually become the B-17. The B-17 also introduced Captain Curtis LeMay to the new world of heavy bombers and would lead to LeMay being posted to the 2nd Bombardment Group (BG), which now flew the new bomber. The 2nd BG would earn fame after its interception of the Italian liner SS Rex on 12 May 1938, during coastal defence manoeuvres by three B-17s, including one navigated by LeMay. This proved the theories of Billy Mitchell, who had passed away two years earlier, and confirmed the importance of developing strategic air power. However, the 2nd BG's interception of the SS Rex only hardened the USNs attitude towards land-based air power and their demands that the USAAC limit their operations to a mere 200 miles (322km) from land were granted for a short period of time.

Eventually the USN had to give ground, and less than a year later President Franklin Roosevelt and Deputy Chief of

The former German battleship *Ostfriesland* is hit by bombing attacks arranged by Mitchell on 21 June 1921. The attacks, which took place near Cape Henry, Virginia (USA) shattered the USNs belief in its invincibility. (USAAC)

Father of the B-29, then Brigadier General Henry Pratt (right), with Brigadier General Benjamin Foulois (left) and Major General James Fechet (centre) in 1931. (USAF)

The Model 294/XB-15 would see service as the XC-105. It is seen here with her crew in Panama in 1943. At the time of its construction the Model 294/XB-15 was the largest aircraft constructed in the US. (Collection of Master Sergeant. Laird N. Rosborough USAAF)

Staff Brigadier General George Marshall were supporting the use and building of long-range air-power assets. Meanwhile Boeing continued to use the XB-15 for developmental work, which would lead to the development of the Model 314 flying boat.

General Henry 'Hap' Arnold, USAAC commander, was convinced that the heavy bomber was the answer to a lot of possible strategic problems. Arnold was foresighted enough to realise that, on taking command of the USAAC in 1938, there was a storm brewing in Europe. As such, the United States had to be prepared to defend itself from European aggression from bases on American soil. At the time, fourteen B-17s were the total strategic heavy bomber force

While the USAAC was planning how to defend American interests, Luftwaffe personnel were gaining combat experience in Spain with the Condor Legion. (Bundesarchiv)

available to him. This situation was further compounded by the fact that there seemed to be little urgency in growing this number, despite huge rearming programmes in Europe.

In January 1939, after reviewing an example of contemporary American air power at Bolling Field, Washington DC, Roosevelt demanded that the United States build '500 bombers a month'. While the call was welcomed, it left Arnold with the decision to identify which bombers he felt best met his need, and that of the USAAC. The first decision made was to call on Consolidated to improve the Boeing B-17, which produced the Model 32; this model would become the B-24. It made its maiden flight on 29 December 1939, giving the Army Air Corps two heavy bombers.

Still not satisfied, Arnold sought a larger VHB, and Brigadier General Walter Kilner was tasked with drafting the specifications.

Roosevelt, who pushed for the development of American air power, enjoys his 61st birthday with his chief military adviser, Admiral William Leahy (to his right) aboard a Pan Am Boeing Model 314 Clipper. Harry Hopkins and aircraft Captain Lieutenant Cone look on. (Museum of the US Navy)

Kilner delivered his findings to Arnold in June 1939 which identified what a future VHB would look like.

Meanwhile, Egtvedt had independently begun to study a similar concept, developing the Model 299 further and creating the pressurized Model 307 Stratoliner. The Stratoliner retained the low-wing design and incorporated a tricycle landing gear. At first Boeing attempted to remodel a pressurized B-17, made from elements of the Stratoliner and B-17 called the Model 322. Trials were unsuccessful, but Boeing had covered its back, so to speak. While developing the Model 322 it had called upon design engineer Lysle Wood to develop a successor aircraft to the XB-15, which would eventually deliver the B-29.

Starting in March 1936 Wood had begun to design the Model 316 using the as yet untested XB-15 as a template. The Model 316 featured a tricycle landing gear and glazed nose, features that would transfer to the serial production B-29. Wood's work was picked up by the USAAC, who gave his study an initial designation Y1B-20. While no orders were made at this stage, Boeing continued to develop the concept, following up with the Model 330 in May 1938 and the Model 333 in January 1939.

The Model 333 was a revolutionary design, utilizing Allison V-1710 engines arranged in pairs, one pushing and one pulling, housed in a shared nacelle. While a unique design feature, Boeing management were quick to recognise future technical issues and the design was refined to the conventional four-engine tractor arrangement. This design would become the Model 333A. As the Allison V-1710 engines were deemed to be inadequate for high-altitude flying, a must for an aircraft of this size, they were swapped for Wright 1800 series engines. The upgraded aircraft, which became the Model 333B, presented Boeing with a further issue: they now had an aircraft in the same class as the B-17 and B-24. The Model 333B was only capable of carrying a one-ton load and had an operational range of 2,500 miles (4023km), leaving Boeing engineers to find a workable solution to improve the design. Their first efforts resulted in the twin-tailed Model 334, which was later mysteriously mirrored by the Messerschmitt Me-264, which first flew three months after the B-29's maiden flight. Thankfully, the Luftwaffe chose not to follow up with the Me-264 until it was too late in the war to make a difference.

The Consolidated B-24 was a highly capable aeroplane, with a reasonable range and bomb load, but for the missions envisaged by Kilner it was not enough. (USAF)

The Boeing Model 307 prototype seen from above. The lineage to the B-29 is taking shape at this stage. (San Diego Air & Space Museum)

Right: The Model 299 (XB-17) on fire after crashing during a test flight at Wright Field. This crash had the potential to stop all heavy bomber development for the USAAC. (USAF)

Below: The German invasion of Poland would show the effectiveness of both tactical and strategic air power. The town of Wieluń, south-central Poland, shown after a Luftwaffe raid on 1 September 1939. (Republic of Poland)

By the summer of 1939 Boeing's engineers were meeting with Material Command staff with the results of their Model 333/334 concepts, hoping to turn their designs into flying prototypes. The groups of engineers presenting alongside Egtvedt included future B-29 chief engineer Edward Wells and Wood, led by Wellwood Beall, vice president in charge of engineering. Army representation included the head of Material Command Colonel Oliver Echols along with Lieutenant Colonels Frank Cook and Donald Putt. Putt was an interesting inclusion in the discussion as he had not only survived the 1935 crash of the XB-17, he was also a keen supporter of the development of strategic air power. Putt

This wonderful contemporary shot of Silverplate B-29 'Straight Flush' gives a hint of the strength of the wing behind the leading edge. 'Straight Flush' would act as weather reconnaissance for the 'Enola Gay' on 6 August 1945. (Todd Cromar/USAF)

would later become the head of production engineering for the B-29. Despite the ongoing meetings, Boeing continued to work on the Model 344 and unveiled the single-tail Model 334A. This was a refinement of all the models between the 316 and the 334, paving the way toward the final B-29 design. On 1 September that year Nazi Germany invaded Poland, triggering the start of the Second World War.

On 2 December 1939, armed with War Department authorization, Arnold's staff began to draft Air Corps Data Request R-40B and specification XC-218. These laid out the specifications for an aircraft with a range of 5,333 milies (8,583km). At the same time Boeing were finishing their full-scale mock-up of a Model 334A and Wells was still developing the concept which would become the Model 341, featuring the distinctive Boeing Model 115 airfoil wing with a span of 124ft 7in (38m). The Model 115 airfoil wing was a game changer; it was exceptionally strong and capable of supporting twice as much weight per square foot than the wings of aircraft before it, including the B-17. The Model 341 was streamlined for maximum efficiency which promised excellent flight performance as there would be no external vents or scoops set into the fuselage. Antennas were streamlined; lightings and de-icing boots were streamlined. Fuselage riveting was set flush to every exterior surface. The aim was to gain speed and advantage through intelligent design and build. On 5 December 1939 Boeing began the engineering mock-up of Model 314.

On 29 January 1940 Boeing, Consolidated, Douglas and Lockheed were sent Air Crops Data Request R-40B to design and build three prototypes of a new long-range heavy bomber. The aircraft would be based on the lessons learned from the development of the B-17 and B-24, with the goal of providing a pressured aircraft capable of high-altitude, long-distance flights. Boeing received their R-40B on 5 February and the task was passed to Philip Johnson, who had taken over as Boeing's president after Egtvedt had been elected to the Board of Directors. This was the second time Johnson had been made president and this time would prove to be the master stroke for the production of the B-29. Johnson's previous roles at Boeing had included being president of United Air Lines, a task which would equip him with the experience to create the necessary production and support structure needed to build the B-29.

Even though Boeing had their wooden mock-up of the Model 334A and the paper draft of the Model 341, their plans were scuppered by new specifications outlined in the R-40B. The request was shaped by combat reports during the first five months of war; the upshot was that a bigger, larger, heavier and more destructive aircraft was needed. This soon started a spiralling battle with weight that would advance the development of the B-29 as the Model 341 simply could not meet it. Engineers began their calculations and lengthened the fuselage a further 6ft (1.8m) to accommodate the necessary changes. Self-sealing fuel tanks and extra defensive armament added to the overall weight; this resulted in the need to carry more fuel, and so the battle raged. The never-ending cycle of increasing weight seemed to be insurmountable with the technology of the day. To help power the increasing weight four Wright R-3350

Johnson's expertise would help B-29s roll off the production lines, but it came at a cost. Three billion dollars would be spent on design and production, a figure dwarfing the Manhattan Project's cost of 1.9 billion dollars. (USGOV-PD)

Changing a Wright R-3350-23 Duplex-Cyclone in field conditions in India. Undamaged elements would be recycled to minimize loss and ensure the B-29s kept flying. (USAF)

A belly view of the Consolidated TB-32 Dominator. This view clearly shows the B-32's B-24 bomb-bay influence. The B-32 would see limited war-time service. (USAF)

An excellent study of Commemorative Air Force B-29 'FiFi' showing off her size. Just visible is the photographer in the port-side gunner's viewing blister, giving an idea of the size of the B-29. (Wallycacsabre)

Cyclone twin-row radial engines replaced the Pratt & Witney R-2800 engines, giving the Model 341 a noticeable increase in power. The 400mph (644km/h) speed demanded by USAAC would be provided by the R-3350s, each with their own turbochargers, giving the B-29 a total of eight. The downside was these engines were new and largely untested on an aircraft of this size. The early R-3350 engines were prone to fires due to overheating as a result of poor air cooling. Ironically, early Tupolev Tu-4s would also experience this phenomenon, which is perhaps testimony to the exactitude of the reverse engineering carried out by the Tupolev team.

Despite the challenges Boeing technicians found the necessary solutions; on 11 May 1940 the drawings for Model 345 were submitted to Material Command. The Model 341 was capable of 5,333 miles (8,583km) and could carry the same bomb load as three B-17s. The Boeing design, which was submitted alongside the Consolidated, Douglas and Lockheed designs, was the one that made Material Command sit up.

Generals George Marshall and Henry Arnold at Quebec, September 1944. Both men would soon be reaping their relative investments in the B-29. (Franklin D. Roosevelt Library, NLFDR)

Development on the B-29 continued. Here a model B-29 is tested for its water-ditching characteristics. (NASA)

General Oliver Echols, chief of the Materiel Division, who would oversee Roosevelt's call for a programme to build 50,000 'military and naval' aircraft per year, designated the new design XB-29. The Lockheed XB-30, a bomber version of the L-49 Constellation and the Douglas XB-31 progressed no further than the drawing board. Consolidated's XB-32 would progress alongside the XB-29 as an insurance policy, should anything go wrong. Eventually, Consolidated would build 118 B-32s, known as Dominators, which would see limited service in the Pacific Theatre from May 1945.

USAAC issued a contract to produce a prototype of the Model 345 on 14 June 1940. As a result, Boeing was awarded a contract for 1,500 aircraft before even producing a single prototype. However, the Model 345 had to be refined and the wind-tunnel, which had helped shape the B-17, was back in service. The main evolution of the subsequent test was the development and strengthening of the Model 115 wing so that it could hold fifty tons. To achieve this task Boeing put their chief aerodynamicist, George Schairer, on to the complex task, which was more than just increasing the wing's overall size. Schairer was more than capable, and as a result produced the Model 117 wing, which added almost another 20ft (6m) to the Model 341's 141ft (43m) wingspan. It also increased the B-29s load-carrying capacity.

Schairer's work resulted in Boeing being awarded a $3.6 million order to produce two XB-29s. With the situation in Europe worsening by the day, and the real possibility that the United Kingdom could fall, thus robbing the USAAC of bases, the need for a long–range bomber was as urgent as ever. The need for Boeing to push through the developmental work and begin building a strategic bomber was never greater. The B-29 was about to become the single largest USAAC programme undertaken.

By April 1941 the wind tunnel tests had been completed, data gathered, with blueprints adjusted as necessary. A full-scale mock-up was constructed and Boeing was able to convince the USAAC that they could have a production aircraft available within three years. After inspecting the plywood mock-up, the USAAC placed two orders on 17 May. The first was for fourteen test airframes, designated YB-29s and 250 serial production B-29s. Such a move was unheard of, yet the sense of urgency demanded this unique situation: an aircraft, which had yet to be flown, was ordered into serial production. The race was on to not only fly the first XB-29 but to create the physical infrastructure and tooling to make the new bomber. The timing could not have been better; Roosevelt was now leaning on the Army Chief of Staff, General George Marshall, and Chief of Naval Operations, Admiral Harold Stark, to build weapons that would defeat Axis forces across the globe. To show how serious he was Roosevelt signed an executive order under the War Powers Act 1941, creating the US Army Air Forces (AAF) on 20 June, two days before the Axis invasion of the USSR. The USAAF was now independent of the Army's General Staff, becoming operationally self-governing; it was placed under the leadership of Arnold.

The first act of Arnold was to appoint a team of exceptional general and staff officers. Their role would be to ensure the new USAAF ran smoothly and to plan

Above left: Brigadier General Haywood Hansell, commanding officer XXI Bomber Command. Hansell's earlier work helped formulate the B-29's strategic role. (USAAF)

Above centre: B-29 Superfortress on the production line. The B-29 went from taking a month to build to less than a week, testimony to the skill of the workforce employed to build this state-of-the-art aeroplane. (USAF)

Above right: Eddie Allen was an exceptional test pilot who had flown some of the largest aircraft built at the time of his death. The employees of Boeing-Wichita bought a B-29 and named it in Allen's honour; it flew twenty-four missions before being written off. (San Diego Air & Space Museum)

ahead, ready for any contingency. General Carl Spaatz became the Chief of Air Staff, an inspired choice. In turn, Spaatz placed Lieutenant Colonel Harold George in the role of leading the Air War Plans Division (AWPD). George and his team were charged by Spaatz to defeat the Axis, powered by whatever means necessary. Victory in the air was now directed by airmen using air power. One of George's team was Major Haywood Hansell, who would become one of the first commanders of the new B-29 force. One of the first tasks of the AWPD was to take the strategic air war to the Germans in Northern Europe, and from there form a plan to defeat Imperial Japanese forces in the east. Hansell helped develop the strategic plan which called for identifying targets of significant importance to the war effort, later replicating this task with Japanese targets, which could only be reached by B-29.

The many discussions that followed resulted in the publication of AWPD-1. This plan called for some 61,500 military aircraft, with the B-29 prominent among them, supported by over two million personnel. The plan was submitted to the Army General Staff on 12 August 1941, with Marshall accepting its contents on 11 September. The ball was now rolling and rolling quickly.

Earlier that summer, to help speed up production of the B-17, Boeing had established the successful Boeing, Douglas and Vega (BDV) Committee. This approach was used for the production of the B-24, so it was inevitable that the B-29 should be produced in the same way. The B-29 Liaison Committee was established on 22 December 1941 and in February 1942 the three key partners, Boeing, Bell and General Motors, met with army representatives to discuss how to build the B-29. Boeing would, understandably, supply all mechanical and technical expertise for the building of the B-29. Boeing also asked for more engineers, especially graduates, which placed them in conflict with the Draft boards, but once the situation had been explained to the Selective Service who ran the boards, Boeing got their staff. General Motors, who had been uneasy in being involved in the project due to other commitments, left the B-29 Liaison Committee, to be replaced by the Glenn L. Martin Company.

On 21 September 1942 test pilot Eddie Allen, considered to be the best in the United States, took the first XB-29 on her maiden flight, after Arnold had placed an initial order for 1,664 B-29s. Regardless of the pressure on Boeing, the flight was a success, but there were concerns with the R-3350 engines. Despite engine failures and fires on the next two flights, Allen continued with testing into 1943 to help solve the issues. On 18 February Allen took off from Boeing's Renton Field in the second prototype with some of Boeing's finest engineers and technicians. Almost two hours after take off a fire started in number one engine and after following the correct procedures, Allen began his return. Soon the entire wing was burning, including the spar, and fifteen minutes after the start of the fire the XB-29 ploughed into the Frye Packing Company building with the loss of thirty lives, including Allen and his crew.

The Frye packing plant on fire, 18 February 1943. (Seattle Post-Intelligencer)

Regardless of the loss, the project moved forward and on 15 April 1943 the first of the YB-29s was rolled out. One of the key changes was replacing the Sperry periscope-sighted gun turrets with General Electric turrets. These were controlled by gunners looking out of side blisters sighted behind the wings' trailing edges. The engines were also upgraded from R-3350-13s to R-3350-21s with the supercharger overheating issue corrected. It had been this which had led to the loss of the second XB-29. The final key visual change was the installation of four-bladed Hamilton Standard propellers. The first flight took place on 26 June from Wichita not long after the third and final XB-29 was been rolled out at Seattle. This aeroplane was used to test the hundreds of changes needed to make the B-29 a war-winning aircraft.

Meanwhile, the AAF had not sat idle and had begun to plan how the B-29 would be used operationally, using the YB-29 as a service test aircraft. It would also be used to train the first crews and further refine the design and numerous systems required to operate the B-29. All of this was going on knowing that the first overseas bases for the B-29 would be in India for operating in the China-Burma-India (CBI) Theatre of operations. Despite the best efforts of all involved the development of the B-29 remained slow, and Arnold tasked Brigadier Kenneth Wolfe with righting the situation and ensuring production expectations were meet. On 15 September Wolf wasted no time and set up his headquarters at Smoky Hill Army Airfield in Kansas, simultaneously activating five Very Heavy Bombardment Groups ready to receive the new aircraft.

By November Roosevelt and Chiang Kai-shek, the Commander-in-chief of the Chinese National Revolutionary Army had agreed on a programme to build airfields, in preparation for the arrival of the B-29s. Meanwhile, Colonel Leonard Harmon of Material Command, who was acting as the B-29 project flight test officer, had started a tick-list of issues that came with the new aircraft. What he was finding was far from reassuring. Aircraft coming from the Modification Centres were often lacking a full inspection and non-standard equipment. By March 1943, two days before B-29s were to begin flying out to the Far East, Arnold visited Smoky Hill to check on progress. The picture was bleak; not a single B-29 was ready.

In what was later called the Battle of Kansas, Arnold isolated the logistical issues and set Major General Bennett Meyers the task of straightening up the situation. Over the next five weeks Meyers cajoled, threatened and bargained his way around the complex logistics' situation. Meanwhile civilian and military technical staff, often working in freezing conditions, worked

A fine study of the forward ventral General Electric gun turret showing its slim-line form. Note the G-1 oxygen bottles beneath the wing spar and the Tokyo Tank in the forward bomb bay. (San Diego Air & Space Museum)

A YB-29 showing off its side and rear ventral gun turrets. The side turrets would be replaced by gunners' plexiglas sighting blisters. (San Diego Air & Space Museum)

themselves to a standstill to make sure all the changes were met. One B-29 was sent to the United Kingdom, not only as a test of its long-range flying capabilities, but also as a propaganda tool.

On 26 March 1944 the first B-29s left for the CBI Theatre. There were issues with engines overheating which was fixed by some exceptional in-field engineering in Egypt, delaying the journey by tewnty-four hours. On 2 April Harmon landed the first of many B-29s to a waiting Wolfe, who had flown ahead four months before, at Chakulia, Calcutta, India. The B-29 had arrived to take the war to Imperial Japan a mere eighteen months after her first flight, testimony to the hard work of all involved in a process that should have taken years. Within sixteen months the war would be over and the B-29 will have become the herald of the Atomic Age.

Superfortress in Detail

The one bonus of the B-29 was its modular design which helped speed up the overall construction process of this complex machine. The flush-riveted fuselage consisted of six separate modules, each fulfilling a particular role. The three pressurized sections consisted of the forward, aft and tail gunner's compartment which sat in the tail section and was partially unpressurized. The two fully unpressurized sections, separated by armoured bulk heads, were the bombbay and wing-spar section. Both could be accessed via a walkway, which could be circumnavigated, between the forward and aft sections of the fuselage, provided the aeroplane was unpressurized and flying below 8,000ft (2,438m).

Once above 8,000ft (2,438m) pressurization would begin, supplied by the onboard engine turbochargers, known as a cabin supercharging system. It also heated the three crewed sections of the B-29. Early aircraft were fitted with petrol-fuelled heaters to maintain cabin heat, though these were replaced by a system which drew heat directly from the turbochargers. Pressurizing and heating the B-29 made perfect sense as missions could take anything up to sixteen hours; this allowed crews to move around unrestricted by heavy flight clothing and biting cold. Pressurization and heating also reduced crew fatigue, vital when on long-range missions over swathes of Japanese territory. Once the aircraft was pressurized the crew could use the 33ft- (10m) long communications tunnel which also housed the navigator's astrodome, close to its

Above: Bunks, Bulkheads and bemusement. This staged shot of the rear pressurized section shows what a quantum leap in development the B-29 was in comparison to the B-17. (USAF)

Right: Not for the faint-hearted. Airman 2nd Class James J. Prater, of the 98th Bomb Wing, moving through the communications tunnel while on a mission over Korea. (NARA)

An excellent study of the Norden Bombsight fitted in the bombardier's position of B-29 'FiFi'. Note the rubber-lined framing. (Azaria E. Foster/USAF)

forward entrance. Throughout the aircraft were intercom connection points, crew oxygen panel points, outlets for heating flying suits and emergency oxygen tanks.

Each section of the pressurized fuselage would house aircrew fulfilling different tasks. The forward section was accessed via a hatch in the front wheel well. It was home to the bombardier, pilots, navigator, flight engineer and radio operator. The bombardier, in keeping with the two-task training regime would be responsible for the lower forward gun turret; this would be operated by the gunners onboard during a bomb run. To aid with bombing, the position was equipped with a Norden Bombsight linked to a Honeywell C-1 autopilot. To aid bombing calculations, the bombardier was given a SCR-718 absolute pulse radar altimeter. This was used to measure absolute altitude in high-altitude bombing, photographic mapping and terrain clearance duties. Operated by the pilot the SCR-718 operates between 50ft (15m) and 40,000ft (12,192m) with an accuracy of roughly 50ft. It would also help establish the bombing altitude. This in turn would work with the bombsight to aid the bombardier in calculating when to release the bombs. This process worked well in continental America, but over Japan, where the winds of the jet stream could reach up to 100mph (161km/h) would interfere with calculations. This in turn led to many targets, especially early in the bombing campaign against the Japanese Home Islands, being missed.

The pilots were relived of much of their work, especially managing the troublesome R-3550 engines by the flight engineer, allowing them to concentrate on the long flights they were making. The flight engineer was responsible for monitoring the engines as well as their fuel flows. On earlier aircraft this was a simple fuel-transfer system which was later changed for a simpler manifold system. Another key responsibility was managing the cowl flaps, which were an almost constant source of trouble. If they were fully opened, they would cause excess drag, if not open enough overheating would occur, possibly leading to an engine fire. The flight engineer's work was a constant, delicate balancing act.

The navigator's role was the same on the B-29 as any other aircraft, but as an additional task the navigator was responsible for the management of the aircraft's five Central Fire Control (CFC) computers. The CFC was also known as the Remote Control Turret System (RCT). This meant keeping them updated with barometric-indicated airspeed and outside air-temperature readings. These were then used to calculate true airspeed, which was also used by the bombardier, and density altitude. This information was

A flight engineer at his station in the B-29 behind the pilots. This role was pivotal in ensuring the success of any mission. (National Museum of the US Air Force)

then sent to all five CFC computers. The final member of the forward compartment team was the radio operator, who ensured all communications systems, including the crew intercom, remained serviceable throughout a mission.

The two bomb bays were divided by the main wing spar, which featured two large boxes, that were eventually utilized to hold fuel cells. The bomb bays were initially fitted with electronically operated actuating screws, but these were replaced by an electro-pneumatic system which could open or close the bomb bay doors in under a second. The space around the main wing spar was also wisely used, with life rafts placed either side of the communications tunnel. Beneath the box were eighteen interconnected Type G-1 oxygen bottles, which provided the crew with oxygen once the aircraft was pressurized. This system was refuelled by a valve situated on the portside of the fuselage forward of the wing root. When fully charged the system could supply the crew with ten hours of oxygen. Alongside the G-1s sat the motor for the AN/APQ-13 ground-scanning radar whose antenna extended downwards externally, where it was shielded by an aerodynamic fairing. The bomb bay could carry a wide range of ordnance. As well as having bomb racks capable of carrying bombs varying in weight from 500Ib (227kg) to 4,000Ib (1814kg), the B-29 could also carry 500Ib bombs on centre racks.

The navigator's station aboard Bockscar. (National Museum of the US Air Force)

The rear pressurized compartment was home to the three gunners' stations, and the radar navigator. The three gunners were able to control all four streamlined turrets, and the tail gun, if need be. Early in the design process it had been agreed that low-drag remotely controlled turrets would be more advantageous than the larger-manned turrets of its predecessors. The other bonus was that by fitting remote-controlled turrets the B-29 would remain pressurized and heated. Each turret was initially fitted with two .50cal machine guns fed by up to 1,000 rounds each. After early combat experiences the upper forward turret received two more .50cal guns from August 1944. Each gunner had a plexiglas blister to look out of, with the upper gunner mounted in what was termed the Barber's Chair. It was also the upper gunner's responsibility to coordinate the action of the others in combat.

At the heart of the B-29's defensive capabilities was the CFC, which was the first such system to be fitted into an operational aircraft, TB-17 and TB-24 training aircraft aside. The five CFCs made three important corrections to accurately aim the aircraft's guns: ballistics, lead and parallax. Initially Bendix, General Electric (GE), Sperry and Westinghouse had stepped forward to design the new CFC. Sperry was chosen as the preferred supplier because of its experience in making analogue fire control and bombing systems. However, like the Consolidated B-32, the Air Corps also tasked GE to develop a system in line with their experience with analogue computers.

Sperry was soon out of the picture as their periscope sights and hydraulic-operated turrets, which were retractable, failed to impress during trials on B-17-equipped testbeds. GE were now handed the baton and they produced a simpler system whereby the gunner tracked the target directly with a sight. Each sight was also given its own CFC which received information from two sight-mounted gyros, known as selsyns, one monitoring the horizontal movement, the other vertical, alongside the ballistic information from the navigator. Once this

Loaded with AN-M64 500lb general-purpose bombs, this shot gives an idea of the size of the B-29's bomb bays. (Platinummedia)

Sergeant D. H. Wood of the Women's Army Corps (WAC) in the B-29's waist gunner's station, which is a stark contrast to the environment gunners in B-17s worked in. (USAF)

Links of .50cal ammunition ready to be loaded. (Lakey, J. Sherrel)

Sergeant Thomas Clark sitting in the Barber's Chair. A great image packed with detail and showing a well-worn fuselage inner liner. (National Archives/Al Schutte)

information was gathered the CFC would then calculate the true air speed and density altitude to make the corrections for ballistics, lead and parrallax. This made defensive gunnery far more effective, as the Japanese would soon learn.

Another interesting aspect of the GE system was the ability for gunners to train more than one turret on a target through an override system. For example, the bombardier was able to control both the upper and lower forward turrets. Each gunner had their own primary turret and in the case of another gunner being unable to fire, a colleague would be able to take control of that gunner's turret. Each B-29 carried two different types of CFC, the 2CH1C1 single-parallax computer, which was used for the nose and tail positions. The 2CH1CD1 double-parallax computer was used by gunners in the aft fuselage station. The system also had two key safety features, a cut-out switch to prevent the gunner hitting his own aircraft, and a deadman's switch which automatically gave control of the individual's turret to another gunner. The effective range of the turrets was 2,700ft (823m) which gave the B-29s' gunners 914 victories against seventy-two losses over some 31,000 sorties flown between August 1944 and August 1945. This should be considered even more remarkable given the system's unreliability, poor build quality and malfunctions, often firing upon friendly aircraft.

The system was gradually removed as the bombing campaign against the Japanese homeland stepped up and speed became more important that defensive measures against a weakened enemy. The system was used, with some success, during the Korean War, where it claimed thirty kills, but the advent of the increasingly faster aircraft made manually laying the guns difficult.

The radar navigator, who was seated behind the gunner's station, was responsible for operating the AN/APQ-13 radarscope as well as early electronic countermeasure (ECM) equipment.

The tail gunner was the last crew member and sat in the partially pressurized tail section, entering via a small, armoured, pressure bulkhead. Once the aircraft was pressurized the gunner was unable to leave his station, making this the most isolated position in the B-29. Originally fitted with twin .50cals and a single 20mm cannon with 125 rounds, the tail gunner's position was well protected with one-inch- (25mm) thick ballistic glass. The 20mm cannon was slowly phased out of production from November 1944 after it was discovered that they were not hitting the same target as the twin .50cals.

It was to be the Wright R-3550 Duplex-Cyclone engines, featuring magnesium crankcases, which would be the B-29's Achilles heel. As the R-3550s were prone to run 'hot' due to their double-stack cylinder design, they would be warm enough to ignite the magnesium. Once ignited, magnesium would burn with a core temperature of 5,600°F (3,100°C), burning through the main wing spar in seconds, leading to the loss of crew and aircraft. Another aspect of using magnesium was that it was brittle, and engines were known to literally fall apart while waiting to take off. The issue was eventually solved by a change in flight tactics, with commanders favouring lower and slower flying. This was the last time magnesium was used in engine construction and its use led to the loss of 267 B-29s to engine fires.

Cooling remained an issue and an investigation by the National Advisory Committee for Aeronautics (NACA) Aircraft Engine Research Laboratory (AERL) at Cleveland, Ohio, raised a series of design flaws. The investigating team soon discovered that the design of the engine's piston heads did not allow for sufficient heat dissipation, resulting in exhaust valve failures. To overcome the issue an elongated cylinder head, with enough surface area to properly disperse the heat was designed. During subsequent wind tunnel evaluations, it was discovered that the engine's exhaust area was being insufficiently cooled. A simple solution saw a cooling air flow directed on the affected area from engine-fitted baffles. At the same time the team were able to redesign the cowl flaps to increase cooling air without causing further drag, making the flight engineer's life a little easier. A further issue was found with the carburettors not distributing fuel evenly to each of the engine's valves. A new impeller design increased the injection flow and created a uniform fuel supply to the cylinders. The baffles and fuel injection impeller increased performance by thirty-eight percent during periods of maximum cooling.

On 22 June 1944 a B-29 was sent to flight test the NACA changes, with the modified engines placed on the port side; test pilots make ten flights using different combinations of the modifications. The flight tests confirmed the NACA studies and showed that with proper fuel mixture and cowl-flap settings the engine was able to attain its maximum range on each flight. With these changes the NACA team estimated that this would give B-29s an extra 10,000ft (3048m) of altitude or allow the carriage of an extra 35,000lbs (15,876kg).

Constructing the Superfortress

Physical production of the B-29 was a complex matter. It was initially hindered by the simultaneous development of the aircraft, a relatively unskilled workforce still learning their crafts and unfamiliar with many of the new technologies that they were working with. Some 50,000 parts made up the B-29, as well as anywhere between 9.5 and eleven miles (15-17.7km)

The radio operator's station onboard 'Bockscar'. (National Museum of the US Air Force)

Airman Second Class Kenneth Roberts of Japan-based 98th Bomb Wing, Far East Air Force (FEAF) Bomber Command, Japan, with his trio of .50cal guns before a mission during the Korean War. (NARA)

of cables, 152 motors, thirteen tons of aluminium, and 1,102lbs (500kg) of copper, all held together by some 600,000 rivets. It was an intimidating task.

The five assembly plants operated by Bell, Boeing and Martin would receive subassemblies from partners in the automotive industry. These included Hudson, who produced rear fuselages, bulkheads and wing sections, and Cessna and the Fisher Body Division of General Motors who produced 13,772 engine nacelles. Dodge (Chrysler) would produce the R-3550 engines and the Hamilton Standard propellers were produced by the Frigidaire Division of General Motors. In total, the B-29 featured some sixty subassemblies.

As was common with all aircraft construction the B-29 was subjected to the block building process. This term related to a group of aircraft which were manufactured to the same specification and configuration. Due to the possible changes that would be required because of user feedback, especially in the early days of the B-29 programme, blocks would be size limited to between fifty and 100 aircraft. This system would not only allow for swift and uninterrupted production but would allow for any specification changes to be gathered together and assessed. This allowed manufacturers to implement changes at the start of each block. It was also easier for the long-term technical and mechanical management, including missed upgrades, of aircraft belonging to a particular production block.

To further ease aircraft identification, especially later when B-29s and their crews operated in field conditions, the blocks were numbered. To help identify the aircraft further, still the individual manufacturing plants code was also added. These details were added to the individual aeroplane's Technical Data Block (TDB) stencilled on the portside of the nose

The troublesome heart; the Wright R-3350 Duplex-Cyclone powered the B-29 in various guises and caused numerous problems early in its use. (Kogo)

The B-29 in NACA Aircraft Engine Research Laboratory's (AERL) Altitude Wind Tunnel in 1944 used to simulate flight conditions at high altitudes, leading to the reduction of drag and improved air flow by reshaping the cowling inlet and outlet. (NASA)

NACA used the B-29 to drop weighted test models from altitudes of 32,808ft (10,000m) to 39,370ft (12,000m) to study aerodynamic forces at transonic and supersonic speeds. (NASA)

Thousands of women answered the call from the production lines to help build the many aircraft wanted by Roosevelt to win the war, affectionately called Rosie the Riveters. (U.S. Office of War Information)

behind the cockpit. The TDB on 'Enola Gay' reads B-29 – 45 – MO, while the TDB on 'Thumper' reads B-29 – 40 – BW. 'Thumper' flew with the 870th Squadron, 497th Bomb Group, Twentieth Air Force. She was the first B-29 to complete forty missions and subsequently returned to the continental United States where she embarked on a bond-selling tour. The final two letters were the code letters given to individual production sites. In total, the five sites and three companies that were involved in the production of the B-29 would build 3,790 units, with the final aircraft rolling off Boeing's Renton production line on 26 May 1946.

The B-29s modular design aided assembly as shown here in this 'exploded' view of the key components. (USAF)

The codes for each plant were:

BO – Boeing Seattle, Washington. This plant only produced the three XB-29s as its main output was the B-17.

BS – Boeing Wichita, Kansas. This site would build 1,630 B-29s from four lines of production.

BN – Boeing Navy, Renton, Washington. The use of the term reflects Renton's original purpose as a site for the building of the Boeing XPBB Sea Ranger. However, the order was cancelled and Boeing was able to produce the B-29 instead. This site would build 1,119 B-29s from four lines of production.

MO - Glenn L. Martin Co, Omaha, Nebraska. This single-line production site would build 531 B-29s.

BA – Bell Atlanta Corps Marietta, Georgia. This site would build 663 B-29s from two lines of production.

Despite the supposed uniformity in the construction of the B-29, one unit found that the rear fuselage of one aircraft, which was to be grafted onto the front of another as a result of combat damage, was slightly larger. This meant that the rear section had to be crimped into place, with the result that the particular B-29 was the fastest in the squadron.

Experimental B-29s

As with all aircraft the B-29 was subject to a period of flying development, needed to shake down the design, identify issues, and produce an aircraft worthy of service. Unlike other aircraft the pressure to develop and deliver an aircraft of unheard-of complexity in a very short period led to the B-29 being developed as it was produced. This was an unheard-of situation; a process that should take years was cut down to months. This led to an almost continuous stream of experimental B-29s leading the development of the AAFs new Very Heavy Bomber.

XB-29

The first of Boeing's experimental B-29s were the XB-92s, with an initial order of two

Wing assemblies at Boeing's Renton Plant. (USAF)

Boeing's three-blade propeller XB-29-BO (S/N 41-002) was the first XB-29 to be built. Note the lack of fuselage turrets. (USAF)

aircraft made in August 1940, followed by a third in December. The first of the three made its maiden flight from Boeing's Seattle plant on 21 September 1941 and, like the other two XB-29s, featured a three-bladed propeller. Testing started immediately and continued until 18 February 1943, when one of the aircraft, the third to be built, flown by experienced test pilot Eddie Allen, caught fire and crashed into the Frye meat-packing plant. The 5,000 gallons of fuel exploded as the XB-29 hit the plant, destroying most of it and killing all eight crew members. The crash and resultant fire killed twenty staff and one fireman.

The crash left Boeing with a huge skills gap, not only was Allen a test pilot par excellence, but he was also chief of the Research Division. The crash investigation was headed by future president Harry Truman, then chair of the Truman Committee, whose role was to reduce waste and inefficiency in military contracts. The subsequent report was scathing and the AAF took back control of the development of the XB-29. Allen's loss was keenly felt, but General Henry Arnold was keen to push on and requested an experienced bombardment pilot to help develop the XB-29. Lieutenant Colonel Paul Tibbets, a veteran of the North African and European theatres was personally recommended by Jimmy Doolitte, then Commanding General of the 12th Air Force in North Africa. Tibbets' input and experience with the B-29 would help during the forming and training of the 509th Composite Group (509 CG) in their delivery of nuclear weapons.

YB-29

A key step in the development of the B-29 was the YB-29 which was built at Boeing's Wichita plant in Kansas. This version brought together all the data and details gathered from the XB-29 programme. The changes were numerous, the main one being the upgrading of the engines from Wright R-3350-13s to R-3350-21s, with the addition of the four-bladed propellers. Fourteen YB-29s were constructed for service testing which included refining the defensive capabilities of the new aeroplane. This led to an improved fire control system powering eight .50cal machine guns spread across four turrets, and a single tail 20mm cannon mounted between two .50cal machine guns.

The YB-29s were used by Boeing and the Army Air Force to help shape the overall design and develop the B-29 into a highly effective aircraft. They gave the aeronautical design and development teams the opportunity to test the effectiveness of their work. For the aircrews working alongside Boeing's civilian teams these aircraft gave them the opportunity to shake down the design, develop the tactics needed for a new kind of air warfare and, most importantly, tailor a training brief.

XB-29E

A single B-29 converted from a standard and used to test new fire-control systems

XB-29G

A converted B-29B used to help test the new jet engines that were steadily coming into air force service. The bomb bay was

Boeing YB-29-BO (S/N 41-36957) with nose-mounted Erco ball turret and twin .50cal machine guns. Further twin .50cal guns are mounted below and aft of the cockpit. (USAF)

modified to fit a cradle, which in turn held the engine to be tested. The cradle could be raised or lowered to allow the engine to be mounted, carried and tested once airborne. The engines carried and tested were the General Electric/Allison J35, which was the first American axial-flow (straight-through airflow) compressor engine. It was also used to test the General Electric J47 and J73, which were tested between 1945 and 1955.

XB-29H

A B-29A modified for armament trials to test configurations.

YB-29J/ YKB-29J/ /RB-29Js

Six B-29s were fitted with the Wright R-3350-CA-2 fuel-injection engines, which in turn were fitted with new Curtiss propellers. Other changes included the fitting of a newly designed cowling known as an Andy Gump cowling. This gave the oil coolers separate air intakes set back from the main cowling engine aperture.

Two of the YB-29Js were later converted to aerial refuelling tanker prototypes, known as YKB-29J, fitted with the new Boeing flying boom refuelling system. The remaining four were converted to fulfil reconnaissance roles, initially as FB-29Js, before being reclassified as RB-29Js. At least one RB-29J saw service with the 91st Strategic Reconnaissance Squadron, 91st Strategic Reconnaissance Wing.

CB-29K

Following other conversions from heavy bombers to transport aircraft, including Boeing's C-108 transport based on the B-17, a single B-29 was converted for use as a freighter. Given that the Model 307 Stratoliner-based C-75 was already in service with the Army Air Force, flying alongside numerous C-47s, the project progressed no further.

XB-39

First flown in 1944, the XB-39, as an experimental XB-39, was fitted with four Allison V-3420-11 liquid-cooled W24 engines, each producing 2,100hp (1,600KWh). The single XB-39 was an insurance development should the proposed serial production engine, the Wright R-3350, be delayed for any reason. Even though it was not fitted with turbochargers, due to delays at General Electric, the first flight on 9 December 1944 proved successful. However, due to its own developmental delays and the operational B-29s now settling into a routine of frontline fixes on their Wright R-3350s the project was cancelled.

B-29

These were the original B-29s with the first rolling off the Glenn L. Martin Company Omaha plant a mere two months after the delivery of the YB-29. These early B-29s were developed in parallel with the testing taking place on the YB-29. Some of the forty-six B-29s were later modified to Silverplate standard for use in delivering atomic weapons.

TB-29 Training Aircraft

As with all new aircraft a trainer is essential to aid crew familiarization and training to ensure successive safe and successful use in theatre. The TB-29 was a simple trainer conversion of either B-29 or B-29A aeroplanes, with all its standard defensive armament removed. This made the TB-29 an effective flying classroom designed to bring future flight crews up to speed on the new Very Heavy Bomber. The TB-29 would also fulfil an auxiliary role in towing two large 45ft (13.7m) targets which were attached to cables that could be unwound from winches mounted in the rear of the aeroplane. The TB-29 would continue to see service after the war, being used as a radar target in the 1950s to help the USAF develop its fighter intercept tactics

B-29A

The B-29A was a development of the early B-29s, with the model produced exclusively by Boeing's Renton Plant, which would serial produce all 1,119 B-29As. The B-29As incorporated a host of changes

XB-29G with its jet engine load raised; note the airman keeping a look out by the tail. (National Museum of the US Air Force)

Left: Boeing RB-29J 'Tiger Lil' and crew from the 91st Strategic Reconnaissance Squadron, 91st Strategic Reconnaissance Wing. (USAF)

which included improved wing design which now saw the wing constructed in three distinct sections as opposed to two. Not only did this strengthen the overall airframe, it also made construction easier. As a result of combat trials an extra two guns were placed in the forward upper dorsal turret. The B-29A ceased production in May 1946.

B-29B

The B-29B was a modification of existing B-29As carried out on 311 airframes by Bell at their Marietta plant in Georgia. The B-29B was intended to fly the long route to the Imperial Japanese Home Islands with the sole intent of carrying out fire bombing. One key modification was the removal of defensive armament and corresponding systems, except for the tail position's two .50cal AN/M2 guns and single 20mm M2 cannon. In time these would be changed to three .50cal AN/M2s. The removal of the remaining defensive armaments gave the lighter B-29B additional speed, increasing the maximum speed from 357mph to 364mph (575km/h to 586km/h). It was felt by senior commanders that this additional speed would help the B-29B evade defending flak.

To aid bombing in overcast situations, an almost continual problem in the early raids against Japanese targets, the B-29B was fitted with the AN/APQ-7 Eagle radar bombsight system, this was further developed to APQ-7A standard which saw the synchronization of the APA-46 and 47 'Nosmo' with the Norden bombsight. The latter system saw little real-time use and was superseded by improved systems after the war.

B-29C

The B-29C was a B-29A fitted with improved Wright R-3350 engines. The Army Air Force had ordered a staggering 5,000 B-29Cs; the war's end saw the order cancelled.

B-29D/XB-44

The final development of the original B-29 design was the B-29D which was fitted with the huge 28-cylinder Pratt & Whitney R-4360-35 Wasp Major engine, producing 3,500hp (2,600KWh) each. In comparison, the B-29A's 18-cylinder Wright R-3350 Duplex-Cyclone engines produced 2,200hp (1,600KWh) each. As a result of the larger engines, the B-29D was given a strengthened wing featuring an enlarged vertical stabilizer. As a result of these changes the B-29D underwent considerable tests with the testing airframe known as the XB-44. Once testing was completed the B-29D became the B-50 and would eventually field a maximum speed of 394mph (634km/h).

The XB-39 seen here at Wright Field, January 1946. The large Allison W24 engines completely change the look of an already big fuselage. (Bill Larkins)

Marines flock around the first B-29 to make an emergency landing at Iwo Jima. (Archives Branch, USMC History Division)

The heritage B-29 'Doc', showing off her plan form, started life as a TB-29 used for radar calibration. (Alan Wilson)

A B-29A photographed at San Francisco in May 1947. (Bill Larkins)

Modification Centres

Throughout the B-29's construction history, especially in the early periods, there were numerous changes which had to be made for the B-29 to be an effective aeroplane. The Block building system helped immensely, allowing manufacturing processes to be refined as experience and confidence in building such an advanced aircraft grew, as well as applying technical changes directly at the production lines. In some cases, vital changes could only be made once an airframe had been constructed. At times changes were so significant that there was a danger in applying them to the blocks already on the production lines as

A B-29B, built by Bell Aircraft at Atlanta, Georgia, ready for delivery. (Bill Larkins)

XB-44 during ground testing of number 3 engine. The new engine nacelles seem cleaner than their predecessors. (USAF)

they would delay a plant's overall output figures. Considering the 20th Air Force's desperate need for B-29s to take the fight to the enemy, a compromise had to be found.

The block system helped immensely as up to 100 aircraft, all produced to the same specifications, could be modified in exactly the same way, thus saving time and money. As there was little room at the five assembly plants, aircraft which has been accepted for service by the Army Air Force were then sent to one of four modification centres to receive their upgrades. This work would result in the aircraft being up to contemporary service standard; aircraft already in service would be upgraded in the field.

Four of the nineteen modification centres available were prioritized for the B-29. The first, operated by the Bell Aircraft Corporation, sat alongside its production plant at Marietta. This was joined by Nr. 8, operated by the Glenn L. Martin Co at Fort Crook, Omaha, Nr. 13, operated by Continental Airways at Denver, Colorado and Nr. 14, operated

The B-29 Superfortress maintenance and modification line at Hill Air Force Base, Utah, 1950. (USAF)

by the Bechtel-McCone-Parsons Corp at Birmingham, Alabama. These centres were staffed by civilians and military technicians who worked hard to ensure each B-29 was ready and capable of fulfilling future missions.

B-29A Specifications

Type: 10-14 crew, Very Heavy Bomber
Engine: four 2,200hp (1641KWh) Wright Cyclone R-3350-23 turbo supercharged radial engines

Performance:
Max Speed: 357mph (575km/h) at 30,000ft (9,144m); cruising speed 220mph (355km/h)
Service Ceiling: 31,850ft (9,708m)
Range with 10,000Ib (4,540kg) bomb load: 3,250 miles (5,230km)

Weight:
Empty: 71,360Ib (32,368kg)
Max. take-off weight: 141,000Ib (64,000kg)
Dimensions:
Span: 141ft 3in (43m)
Length: 99ft (30.2m)
Height: 27ft 9in (8.5m)
Wing Area: 1,739ft^2 (161.3m^2)
Armament: 10 x .50cal machine guns, 1 x 20mm cannon and 20,000Ib (9,072kg) of bombs
Total Produced: 3,970

Superfortress in Service

Although introduced late into the war, it was felt that the B-29 would be better utilized in the Pacific, as the air war over Europe was now very clearly in its end game. The B-29, like its smaller sibling, the B-17, was a tough aircraft capable of getting crews home after absorbing a huge amount of punishment. As a new aircraft it presented both new and converting pilots with a challenge, including the high-wing loading.

Corporal John Green working on the engine of a weather-beaten B-29. (NARA)

From flying the large aircraft to operating its many systems, the B-29 was as complex as it was large and each member of the ten-man crew had to know their role and perform it flawlessly to ensure operational efficiency.

Once bases had been established, first in India and China, and then in the wake of the advancing allied forces in the Pacific, the B-29 got to work. As the B-29 could carry a load of up to 10,000lbs (4,540kg) it packed a considerable punch. Post war the B-29 continued to play its part as a strategic asset in the USAAF/USAF inventories and was found to be an aircraft capable of fulfilling a range of roles. From air-to-air refuelling to carrying out reconnaissance tasks as well as the ubiquitous bombing role, the B-29 had become a stalwart symbol of the newly formed Strategic Air Command. The Korean War would become the B-29s swansong, as the jet age produced a new generation of faster and deadlier fighter aircraft that the B-29 could simply not fend off.

While no longer a front-line aircraft the B-29 continued to contribute to the development of the next era of aviation, acting as mother ship to a range of aircraft including the record-breaking Bell X-1. Despite being officially retired, from operational flying, with the USAF on 21

An interesting period photo showing B-29 'Enola Gay' at the Oklahoma City Air Depot. Note the 'Fat Man' markings. (Tinker Air Force Base History Office archives/ Defense Visual Information Distribution Service

June 1960, a few KB-50s and WB-50s would continue to flying until 1965.

The B-29 has more than earned its place in the halls of aviation fame. It was an aircraft ahead of its time that helped usher in a new age of military aviation and provides a tangible bridge between new and old ways.

Second World War

Making its maiden flight on 21 September 1942 and introduced into service on 8 May 1944, it was felt the B-29, with its long-range capabilities, would be better utilized in the Pacific theatre. It could absorb a huge amount of punishment from enemy fire, as well as the almost inevitable mechanical issues. As one of the last piston-powered aircraft the B-29 presented pilots with challenges brought about by a range of technical innovations. From flying the large aircraft to operating its many systems, the B-29 crew had to know its role inside out, often in a very short period of time, especially in its early days of use.

The first major step was to ascertain who would command the new B-29 force. In Europe General Dwight Eisenhower had overall control of the four army air forces, while General Douglas MacArthur commanded the three air forces of the Pacific Theatre. General Arnold recognized that in these situations air power was predominantly tactical, and the B-29 was very much a strategic asset. Therefore, they needed to be commanded as a separate entity, and their use focused on the defeat of Imperial Japan. As such, a new air force was established, the Twentieth, which was commanded by led by General Henry Arnold under the watchful eye of the Joint Chiefs of Staff. The Twentieth Air Force was activated on 4 April 1944. It would not only fly the B-29 but would be the sole operator of the B-29 for the duration of the war.

As part of its organization three Bomber Commands (BC) were planned for the Twentieth. XX Bomber Command was to be based in the CBI Theatre, XXI Bomber Command in the liberated Pacific islands and XXII Bomber Command in the Philippines, though this was later cancelled. As the Twentieth came under Army control, and the war in the Pacific was being led by soon-to-be Fleet Admiral Chester Nimitz, old rivalries soon reared their heads. However, sense prevailed, and the Navy gave the Twentieth, and more importantly Arnold, the space it needed, though there would be the odd clash.

The first B-29s arrived in India belonged to the 58th Bombardment Operational Training Wing, Heavy, on 2 April 1944. The 58th, founded on 11 September the previous year, now found its aircraft forming the nucleus of XX Bomber Command, with Major General Kenneth Wolfe as its commander. Before the battle could be taken to the Japanese, bases would have to be built in China. To help aid construction

Raids could be rough, but the B-29 proved itself to be a remarkably tough aeroplane, as seen here. (Unknown)

A KB-29P of 420 Air Refuelling Squadron based at RAF Sculthorpe, Norfolk during an open day proves that the B-29 was not only adaptable, but also durable. (RuthAS)

of the runways needed, Chiang Kai-shek had mobilized tens of thousands of Chinese workers to help build them. This led to the first B-29 missions being that of cargo carriers rather than bombers, helping to build the runways needed until suitable Pacific islands could be liberated.

What followed was known as Operation Matterhorn, with young and often inexperienced crews making the hugely treacherous flight over the Himalayas, known as the Hump, from four airfields in India to four airfields in China. The flights

Mothering in the new age. A B-29 mothership with the Bell XS-1 experimental rocket-powered research aircraft. (NASA)

needed to supply a single raid were never enough and logistics, another thorn in the B-29's side, saw fuel and bombs arrive, in small numbers.

The stresses upon the early crews, who were simultaneously developing a weapons platform, the tactics needs to fulfil their strategic role, and making stressful long-distance flights, must have been immense.

The first combat mission followed, with a strike on the Makasan rail yard near Bangkok, Thailand, on 5 June 1944. Ninety-nine B-29s were scheduled to make

Band of Brothers, the crew of the 'Coral Queen' seen here at Saipan. (USAF)

'Eddie Allen' preparing for take off. The four camels on the fuselage side indicate how many flights it had flown over the Hump as part of Operation Matterhorn. (USAF)

Operating in the CBI Theatre was hard, the hours long and the facilities basic, with all personnel lending a hand to construct accommodation and prepare the way for operations. (Signal Corps Archive/US Army)

the raid, with sixty-four completing it. The results were far from satisfactory, but they were a start, and soon raids were leaving China for Imperial Japanese targets, including one of the Japanese Home Islands, Kyushu. As the raids continued the young, inexperienced crews found their feet, battling weather, technical issues and a tenacious enemy.

These factors would have an effect on operational efficiency, but the XX BC's newly arrived commander, Major General Curtis LeMay, was determined to see improvements. LeMay had arrived, straight from the Eighth Air Force in Europe on 29 August 1944, to replace Wolfe. LeMay hit the ground running, introducing new tactics, better suited to strategic bombers, and increasing flying hours to ensure all crew members were confident in their roles. This helped LeMay establish what the B-29 was really capable of.

Meanwhile, the advancing Allied forces were driving ever closer to the Japanese Home Islands, and in October 1944 XXI BC arrived at Saipan, making their first raid on 28 October. XXI BC was commanded by Major General Haywood Hansell Jr, who had been one of the chief architects of strategic daylight precision bombing. XXI BC's arrival at Saipan now put Tokyo in reach of the B-29; early reconnaissance by an F-13 of the 3rd Photographic Reconnaissance Squadron delivered 7,000 stills of the Imperial capital. This was followed by further reconnaissance missions and the first raid launched from the island, with 111 B-29s taking off. It was also the first time the Americans encountered the Jet Stream, which passed over the Japanese Home Islands. This affected bombing accuracy and the maintenance of flight formations. Despite the disappointing results and continued Japanese attacks against its home base at Saipan, the XXI BC continued its attacks, though the results remained negligible.

On 20 January 1945 LeMay left XX BC to wind down its operations in the CBI Theatre and took command of XXI BC. By early March Iwo Jima had fallen to Allied troops, affording the XXI a mid-way emergency landing site and a home for their P-51 escort fighters. At the same time the Mariana Islands were fully under American control, with Tinian home to the 58th and 313th Bomber Wings, Guam home to the 314th and 73rd at Saipan. With all the pieces in place LeMay was now able to introduce his first key change, the introduction of fire bombing.

As the B-29 could carry a load of up to 10,000lb (4,540kg), it packed more than a considerable punch and no where was this better demonstrated than on the first Tokyo raid of 9-10 March 1945 during Operation Meetinghouse. The results were terrifying, 16 square miles (41km^2) of Tokyo were razed; the loss of life was over 100,000, with a million left homeless. It was the single most destructive bombing raid in history. The raids against Japanese targets gradually increased, and soon the B-29s began laying naval mines to disrupt and destroy Imperial Japanese naval assets.

On 12 April 1945 President Franklin Roosevelt died and Vice-President Henry Truman became the 33rd President of the United States. On 25 April Truman was briefed on the Manhattan Project which, up to that point, he had no awareness of. Truman was also briefed on the existence of the 509th Composite Group commanded by Colonel Paul Tibbets, flying its special Silverplate B-29s.

Operations in the run up to the planned land invasion of the Japanese Home Islands in 1946 were now reaching a crescendo, so when the 509th arrived at Tinian very little notice was paid. The 509th started training flights and operational sorties using high-explosive-filled Pumpkin Bombs against Japanese targets to get used to delivering their special weapons. On 25 July General Carl Spaatz, now the commander of the US Strategic Air Forces in the Pacific, gave the 509th the go ahead to mount their attack against targets on the Japanese Home Islands. This order would culminate in the dropping of nuclear bombs on the cities of Hiroshima on 6 August and Nagasaki on 9 August 1945.

On 15 August 1945 Emperor Hirohito announced the surrender of the Empire of Japan. This was formally signed at 0923 on 2 September 1945 aboard the *USS Missouri* in the Bay of Tokyo, by Japanese Foreign Minister Mamoru Shigemitsu, representing the Emperor of Japan, thus ending the Second World War.

Korean War

Post war the B-29 continued to play its part as a strategic asset in the USAAF/USAF inventories as a nuclear-capable bomber. It was also found to be an aircraft capable

Above: B-29s of the 29th Bombardment Group assembling at the North Field in Guam, 1945. By now LeMay had the numbers he needed to start hitting Imperial Japanese targets hard. (USAF)

Above: The crew of 'Hollywood Commando', 677th Bomb Squadron, 444th Bomb Group, XX Bomber Command, at Kwanghan Airfield (A-3), China, 11 November 1944. (USAAF)

Above: The 'Enola Gay' landing after the atomic bombing of Hiroshima on 6 August 1944.

Left: Luis Alvarez wearing his body armour in front of Silverplate B-29 'The Great Artiste', 393nd Bomb Squadron, 509th Composite Group. (US Govt)

A great profile study of a Strategic Air Command KB-29M at Oakland Airport, California, 1952. (Bill Larkins)

'Its Hawg Wild' served with 371st Bombardment Squadron, 307th Bomb Group, 307th Bomb Wing at Kadena, Okinawa from March 1952. She flew 105 combat missions over North Korea. (Alan Wilson)

Staff Sergeant Arthur Goins loading one of the six cameras carried on the RB-29, in this case flown by 31st Strategic Reconnaissance Squadron. (NARA)

of fulfilling a range of roles. From air-to-air refuelling to carrying out reconnaissance tasks and its ubiquitous bombing role, the B-29 had become a stalwart symbol of the newly formed Strategic Air Command.

On 25 June 1950 the North Korean People's Army poured across the 38th parallel, the boundary between the Soviet-backed Democratic People's Republic of Korea to the north and the pro-Western Republic of Korea to the south. The B-29 was now much reduced in numbers with most types based on continental United States. Early tasks saw WB-29s carrying out reconnaissance missions and SB-29s providing valuable air-sea rescue tasks. The first bombing raid, made by the Guam-based 19th Bombardment Group, took place on 29 June against railway targets at Kimpo and Seoul. Despite the defenders' best efforts, the tide of the North Korean advance seemed unstoppable and Far East Air Force (FEAF) commander Lieutenant Colonel George Stratemyer requested reinforcements.

Eventually two Bombardment Groups arrived in theatre, the 22nd and 92nd joined the 19th. Two BGs would fly tactical support, guided by a Forward Air Controller (FAC), and the third would act in the strategic role. It was soon clear that the B-29 remained suited to the strategic role and tactical use was soon limited to actions between the front line and the 38th Parallel. The new strategic campaign would see the 19th BG utilize the VB-3 Razon-guided bombs. Between 23 August and December 1950 several hundred were used against bridges, and while crews enjoyed some success against targets, the Razon lacked the necessary punch to be a fire-and-forget weapon and crews were soon using the heavier VB13/ ASM-A-1 Tarzon. The Tarzon was first used on 15 January 1951 but by early March its use had been suspended due to a host of technical issues, with its use formally abandoned on 13 August. On 6 July KB-29M tankers from 43rd Air Refuelling Squadron (ARS) made the first combat air refuelling mission, marking a key development for the B-29 and its variants.

By the summer the bombing focus had shifted once more, with airfields becoming the primary target of the B-29. Meanwhile, industrial targets in North Korea would become the focus of operations like those used over Japan. This required more B-29s and by late summer the 98th and 307th BGs had arrived in theatre, making their operational debuts on 7 and 8 August respectively. On 30 August a B-29 was employed to drop flares to help support operations undertaken by a sortie of B-26s. The mission was a success and soon B-29s, armed with flares and bombs, were supporting night operations. This was especially important during Operation Chromite, the amphibious assault on Inchon and the subsequent breakout from Pusan.

The Chinese People's Volunteer Army's (PVA) entry into the war on 19 October 1950 meant a well-equipped, well-trained, and highly motivated adversary. Soon Chinese Mig-15s swarmed the skies, with them came highly effective Chinese Anti-Aircraft Artillery (AAA). The PVA operated completely differently to the North Koreans, often moving at night; by the spring of 1951 the weather further complicated the effective interception of lines of communication. To help overcome the situation Short Range Navigation (SHORAN), a type of electronic navigation and bombing system, was deployed. SHORAN required AN/APN-3 Airborne Navigation Radars and two AN/CPN-2 or -2A ground stations. The equipment carried by the B-29 consisted of a transmitter, receiver, an indicator and a K-1A bombing navigational computer. Integrating the K-1A with the navigation system produced the SHORAN guidance system which delivered reliable and accurate blind-bombing.

Despite the presence of effective Chinese air defence the B-29 continued to be used in daylight, but the growing presence of MiGs saw the B-29 relegated to night attacks from 23 October 1951. The Chinese and North Koreans were quick to adapt, but the B-29's crews and commanders were equally quick and by the beginning of 1953 B-29s were deployed in smaller numbers, with extensive Electronic Countermeasure (ECM) and fighter support.

When the United Nations Command reached an armistice with China and North Korea on 27 July 1953, fifty-seven B-29s had been lost, but they had a tally of over thirty enemy aircraft kills including some sixteen MiGs. By war's end the B-29s had flown a total of 20,000 sorties and dropped 180,000 tons of ordnance. These aircraft included B-29A 'Command Decision', which shot down five MiG-15s, unofficially making it a bomber ace. 'Command Decision' also flew an astonishing 121 missions in over 1,500 combat hours, dropping 2.5m/lbs of ordnance (1,1m/kg).

B-29s fly towards an enemy target. Missions such as this were vital in supporting United Nations forces in the early stages of the Korean War. (NARA)

An RB-29 of the 31st Strategic Reconnaissance Squadron flying over Korea during the opening phases of the Korean War. (NARA)

A VB13/ ASM-A-1 Tarzon was a radio-controlled bomb based on the British 12,000lb Tallboy designed by Barnes Wallis. (Unknown)

Airman Second Class Don Murray of the 307th Bomb Wing in his gun position celebrating his kill, that of an enemy jet aircraft. (NARA)

Above: Gunner Benjamin Livingston of 98th Bomb Wing adjusts his sights in preparation for action. (USAF)

Chinese Mig-15s were often flown by seasoned Soviet Pilots, including Nikolai Sutyagin. This meant that the MiGs were restricted to flying over North Korean airspace lest the pilot's cover be blown. (Ad Meskens)

Below: Mechanics of the FEAF inspecting one the B-29's four R-3350 surrounded by bombs and their tail fins at an undisclosed airfield during the Korean War, most likely Japan, given the lack of security. (NARA)

Superfortress Variants

Boeing's B-29 platform was exceptionally flexible, with the design giving rise to a host of variants, from training aircraft to search-and-rescue aircraft, as well as influencing future aircraft designs. Like the earlier B-17, the B-29 series of aircraft followed the Boeing tradition of innovation, testament to the ingenuity of its design and development teams, as well as to the men and women who flew, fought, and serviced her. Capable of withstanding enormous punishment, the B-29 was very much a project in progress with Boeing and the Army Air Force, as learning took place as they went along. The B-29 also helped to usher in the next generations of aircraft design and innovation, including space flight, earning it a place as a true legend of aviation history.

United States

As the primary operator of the B-29 it's hardly surprising that the Army Air Force (AAF) developed the aeroplane to the fullest. This not only showed the inbuilt flexibility of design which had become a Boeing hallmark, but also the ingenuity of the designers in adapting the bomber's airframe to fulfil a wide range of the roles.

American military aviation prefixes nomenclature changed during the period of the B-29s service. The prefixes used in the following variants were used by the USAF between 1948 and 1962. These ran until the 1962 introduction of the Tri-Service aircraft designation system which was based on the USAF 1948–1962 system.

Silverplate/Saddletree

One of the first major variants of the B-29 was the Silverplated Project or Silverplate series of conversions which was carried out as part of the AAFs contribution to the Manhattan Project. The nickname Silverplate was initially chosen to refer to B-29s converted for use as nuclear-weapon-carrying aircraft, but was soon extended to nuclear-related B-29 activities. Initial tests and developments were carried out on scale models at Naval Proving Ground, Dahlgren, Virginia in August 1943. By November all parties had gained enough information to convert the first B-29, referred to as 'Pullman', in preparation for flight testing. 'Pullman' would further develop the aircraft's modifications and use as a bomber from March 1944 at Muroc Army Airfield, California.

The ever-evolving B-29 soon lost its cumbersome 20mm rear gun, occasionally replaced by a third .50cal. (Unknown)

'Little Boy' in the pit before loading into 'Enola Gay's' bomb bay at Tinian, note the bomb bay door. (NARA)

In August 1944 seventeen Silverplate specification B-29s were ordered from the Martin Omaha Modification Centre for use by the 509th Composite Group, formed specially to deliver nuclear weapons. The 216th Army Air Force's base unit worked alongside the 509th to carry out future ballistic testing work, known as Project W-47, at Wendover Army Airfield, Utah. Twenty-eight more conversions were ordered in February 1945, which included the infamous 'Enola Gay' and 'Bockscar'. The key changes to the B-29 included the removal of all defensive armaments and fuselage sighting windows, except the tail guns. An additional fuel tank was fitted in the aft bomb bay; the forward bomb bay was equipped to carry the nuclear payload. There was also now a crew member responsible for managing the onboard nuclear weapon, known as the Weaponeer, placed in the radio operator's position. The radio operator was placed opposite the radar operator in the aft cabin space.

Alongside the B-29's conversions was the development of the specialist bombs, the Thin Man and Pumpkin (Fat Man) nuclear bombs. These were initially conceived in December 1944 by United States Navy (USN) Captain William Parsons, head of the Ordnance Division at the Los Alamos Laboratory, and commander of the 509th, Lieutenant Colonel Paul Tibbets.

Thin Man bombs were designed as plutonium gun-type nuclear weapons, but these were found unsuitable, and the design was abandoned in July 1944. During the design process it was discovered that the spontaneous fission rate of nuclear reactor-bred plutonium was too high for use in a Thin Man gun-type bomb due to the high concentration of the isotope plutonium-240. Some of the design work would be used for the enriched uranium gun design that became known as Little Boy. This weapon looked like an aerial mine, so much so that the USN would construct a further twenty-five Little Boy assemblies, despite most plans relating to the design being destroyed post war, for use in its Lockheed P2V Neptune anti-submarine warfare (ASW) fleet.

Five casings of the Little Boy would be made to help crews with loading and arming drills as well as to provide further carriage chassis should the need arise. Despite its success at Hiroshima, the design was far from perfect, but due to Plutonium shortages six assemblies were made at the nuclear weapons installation of Sandia Base, New Mexico, to fill any strategic need. The Little Boy series of nuclear weapons would use the Marman Clamp while being carried by Silverplate B-29s. The Marman Clamp was a quick-disconnect connector which had been designed by engineer and comic Zeppo Marx.

The Pumpkin (Fat Man) nuclear bombs were developed alongside Thin Man/Little Boy and were designed to deliver a more effective implosion-type plutonium-based explosion. The large bulbous shape housed a complex assembly which shrouded the plutonium core. A series of conventionally filled five-ton Fat Boy bombs were used operationally on a range of sites, including Nagasaki, to get crews used to the new tactics required with the weapons delivery.

As Project Alberta developed nineteen more Silverplate B-29s were ordered in July 1945 which were delivered between the end of the war and the end of 1947. The use of the nickname Silverplate was discontinued after it was compromised, but modifications continued under a new nickname, Saddletree, including an in-flight refuelling capability. A further eighty aircraft were modified under this programme. The last group of B-29s was modified in 1953 but did not see service before the B-29 was withdrawn from the Strategic Air Command inventory.

Deak Parsons (right) supervizes loading 'Little Boy' into 'Enola Gay'. (NARA)

The crew of the 'Enola Gay' either side of Paul Tibberts Jr (with pipe). (USAF)

Thin Man bomb casings developed as part of Project Albert. The design was discontinued as it was deemed unfeasible. (Los Alamos/Manhattan Project)

Guardian Angel/ Porcupine B-29 Electronic Countermeasures Aircraft

The B-29 was quickly adapted to fulfil the role of providing Electronic Warfare solutions for the Twenty-first Bomber Command B-29s operating from the Mariana Islands. While the air force had access to two B-24 Liberator 'Ferret' radar hunters, the B-29 gave the Twenty-first Bomber Command an aircraft that could be deployed alongside those B-29s on their long-range missions. Technicians soon put the eleven miles of electronic cabling each B-29 carried to good use, to combat the Japanese radar systems copied from captured Allied sets and used by anti-aircraft defences, including directing Nakajima J1N1 Gekkō night fighters.

The extra ECM equipment replaced the crew bunks, where fitted, in the aft pressurized compartment. The operator, who had not been factored into Boeing's original crew planning, was perched on the chemical toilet. Thankfully only a few B-29s needed an ECM operator to carry out spot jamming with an onboard AN/APQ-2 high-power barrage-jamming transmitter. This meant that the other B-29s' ECM suites and systems were operated by the radio operator.

The ECM-equipped B-29s started supporting operations in early 1945 and were equipped with an impressive ECM suite which included ten pre-tuned AN/APT-1 or AN/APT-3 band spot-jamming radar transmitters fitted in the forward bomb bay. These were augmented by three spot-tuned AN/APT-1 or AN/APT-3 radar transmitters, which were operated by up to two crew members against specific targets. With all this equipment the rear section of the B-29 fuselage became a profusion of antenna masts, leading to the nickname Porcupine. These aircraft soon developed their own tactics against targets with four Porcupines tracing patterns at differing heights. These aircraft would fly in either a clockwise or anti-clockwise orbit over the target area, depending on their position, with the lowest starting clockwise.

Alongside the ECM equipment the Porcupines also dropped RR-3/U rope chaff, which was deployed via automatic dispensers by the radio operators, as well as VHF jamming of Japanese radio signals. These were initially highly successful, but Electronic Intelligence (ELINT) staff at all levels soon protested as they were unable

Two of the original five Little Boy bombs with part of their casings removed, showing the internal mechanisms of the devise. (Manhattan Project)

Fat Man being placed on its trailer cradle in front of Assembly Building at Tinian. This photograph gives a great indication of how big the Pumpkin Bomb was. (War Department/Office of the Chief of Engineers/Manhattan Engineer District)

to make recordings of Japanese air defence radio traffic. This led to an order for VHF jamming to cease, much to the shock of the aircrew taking part in missions which benefitted from jamming.

B-29F

Six B-29s were converted for cold-weather operations in Alaska based at Fort Wainwright AFB. Of the six, one B-29F

The B-29 continued to be used in the development of atomic weapons. Here a radioactive B-29, which has been used in the Atomic bomb tests at Nevada Proving Grounds on 21 April 1952, is being decontaminated at Indian Springs Air Force Base, Nevada. (National Nuclear Security Administration)

A KB-29P losing fuel through its fully extended flying boom. The apparatus below the tail is the housing for the drogue basket, used with probe-equipped aircraft. (USAF)

would be lost after a post-take-off crash on 29 May 1947. The remaining five would be converted back to standard B-29 fit.

KB-29 Tanker Aircraft

Based in the United States and North Africa the KB-29 series of aircraft were designed to provide larger multi-engine aircraft with much-needed fuel on longer missions, especially Strategic Air Command-based B-29s and B-50s working in the nuclear deterrence role. Boeing would produce two types of refuelling aircraft: KB-29M and KB-29P.

The first tanker was the KB-29M, converted from ninety-two B-29s and used to refuel the B-29MR long-range bomber. Using the British system of dropped lines and hooks, the KB-29M had all armaments, turrets and fire control systems removed, and it's bomb bay fitted with an auxiliary 2,300-gallon (10,456l) fuel tank for carrying fuel for re-fuelling tasks. The tank was also part of the overall fuel system enabling fuel to be transferred to the KB-29M if needed. The KB-29M was fitted with a system of hoses, reels, winches and pumps required for the transfer of fuel to the waiting B-29MR. The KB-29M was fitted with a power-driven reel for the refuelling hoses and lines needed to complete the refuelling process; these were fed out though the lower rear turret position. Some KB-50s were also fitted with this system, with hoses mounted in under-wing pods and used by first generation jet aircraft, especially the smaller fighters.

Although the hose refuelling system proved to be feasible, it took time to set up and, once the hosing was connected, which added to aerodynamic drag, the fuel transfer rate was slow. Consequently, the hose system was used for only a few years before it was replaced by the Boeing-developed flying boom system. Several KB-29Ms were modified to carry the probe-and-drogue system.

The KB-29M was followed by the KB-29P which used Boeing's rigid flying boom system mounted underneath the rear gunner's position. The boom is attached to the aircraft by a universal joint which also allows for pitch and yaw movements. One notable feature of the boom is its V-tail, known as a Ruddervator, which can be controlled, allowing the operator to make adjustments to the boom and help manoeuvre it into position. The rigid flying boom system would also allow the USAFs

A KB-29P at Keesler AFB Armed Forces Day, May 1954, from 508th Air Refuelling Squadron showing the flying boom in its stowed position below the drogue basket housing. (Tequask)

A fine close-up of a North American RB-45C of the 323rd Strategic Reconnaissance Squadron, 91st Strategic Reconnaissance Wing being refuelled by a 91st Air Refuelling Squadron Boeing KB-29P. (USAF)

burgeoning fighter fleet to extend its range in the air. Eventually the rigid flying boom system would become the main refuelling system for American military aircraft.

B-29L/B-29MR (Modified Receiver) Long Range Aircraft

Initially designated the B-29L, the B-29MR was the designation given to seventy-four B-29s converted for possible long-range attacks on Soviet targets with nuclear weapons. The B-29MR conversion entailed removing all the gun turrets and fire control system but keeping the tail gunner's position in place. Some B-29MRs had their left and right gun sighting blisters removed and replaced with flush fitted 25.4mm (10in) windows to help reduce drag. The rear bomb bay received a 2,300gal fuel tank, while the forward bomb bay was modified to carry a nuclear payload. In addition the B-29MR was fitted with AN/APN-2B and AN/APN-68 radar equipment to aid with its in-flight liaison of the KB-29M.

The system was complex and became a highly skilled task. When carried out it worked, but only just. The famous B-50 'Lucky Lady II' was fitted to MR standards to enable in-flight refuelling during her 1949 non-stop flight around the world. Some B-29MRs would be modified with an external probe mounted on the Port side of the fuselage over the captain's position in the cockpit to utilize the probe-and-drogue system.

GB/EB-29 – Exempt Aircraft used as 'X' Project Motherships

The EB-29s were developed as carrier aircraft with modified bomb bays tailored to bear experimental aircraft as a mothership. These included the initial testing of Bells X-1 rocket-powered supersonic research aeroplane flown by Chuck Jaeger and the McDonnell XF-85 Goblin parasite fighter aeroplane. The Bell series of rocket-powered aircraft would later be carried by a converted B-50, and the Goblin would be tested for release and capture from a specially designed trapeze fitted RB-29B mothership. Sadly, the B-50 mothership would be destroyed by a fire which took place while the X-1-3 was being refuelled after a flight.

The RB-29B would continue to test the Goblin, designed to protect its mothership over enemy territory, for carriage by the Convair B-36, its intended operational carrier. The Goblin was hampered, understandably, by its short range and demanding flight characteristics. After the project was cancelled an EB-29A would assist in further tests including Project MX-1016 (Tip-Tow).

Project MX-1016 would see the mothership, known as ETB-29 carry two Republic EF-84D Thunderjets, with the provision for in-flight attachment/detachment of the fighter to the bomber via wingtip connectors. During flight the EF-84Ds would be manually controlled by their pilots and would fly with their engines switched off. Initial tests proved promising, and Republic was contracted to develop automatic flight control modifications. Unfortunately, on 24 April 1953, after hooking up with the mothership and activating its automatic flight control modifications the EF-84D immediately flipped over onto the ETB-29's wing, leading to the loss of both aircraft and five personnel.

B-29 Photo Reconnaissance Aircraft

The chain of command was quick to utilize the range of the B-29s in the role of reconnaissance, especially checking the

Hose-and-Drogue equipped KB-29M refuels a KB-29MR fitted with the nose probe. (USAF)

An EB-229 with its X-1B attached taxis in 9 April, 1958. (NASA)

EB-29A seen here docked wingtip-to-wingtip with its two EF-84Ds for Project Tip-Tow. (USAF)

weather over planned targets. One-hundred-and-eighteen B-29s were initially modified for reconnaissance and carried three K-17B, two K-22 and one K-18 cameras. These would be referred to as F-13/F-13A, with the F standing for photo. After the war these aircraft would be designated as FB-29J, this term would be changed once more in 1948 as remaining F-13 and FB-29s received the new designation RB-29 and RB-29A. Some RB-29s would be fitted with specialist equipment such as radars and communications intercept suites to carry out and record highly secretive Electronic Intelligence (ELINT) and Communications Intelligence (COMINT) tasks. The latter role was done as part of the mission of the Air Force Security Service (AFSS).

These aircraft, known a Ferrets, would eventually work around the globe, carrying six electronic warfare officers among the thirteen crew and would see service in the Korean War. Three would be lost in action in Korea and a further three would be lost in International waters after being intercepted by Soviet aircraft.

WB-29 Weather-Monitoring Aircraft

In 1946 the AAF Air Weather Service (AWS) was established to provide accurate weather reporting to support military operations. Initially the new service had forty-six specially equipped RB-29s, which would carry the weather officer. Airborne dropsonde sensors were ejected from the RB-29 via a special ejection chamber and were controlled by a dropsonde operator. The dropsonde sensor is an expendable weather reconnaissance device suspended underneath a parachute designed specifically to be dropped over water. It includes a suite of on-board features which measure temperature and humidity.

As well as weather reconnaissance equipment the RB-29 would also carry an extra 640gal (2,423l) fuel tank in each bomb bay to help extend range as well as

The F-13 that carried Major Maynard White, commander of the 46th Reconnaissance Squadron, and crew, as well as military scientists, over the North Pole. (NARA)

RB-29A with ELINT fit. Note the rear fuselage antennas. (San Diego Air & Space Museum)

The crew of this WB-29 tracked the radioactive clouds resulting from atomic detonations at the Atomic Energy Commission's Nevada Proving Ground during 1952 nuclear tests. (US Navy)

A modified B-29 was used by NASA as a flying laboratory by its Aircraft Engine Research Laboratory. Here it's in use recording high altitude flight data to determine what conditions cause ice to form on wings and aircraft surfaces. (NASA)

a new radar system, a radar altimeter, and improved communications systems. Other features included an atmospheric sampling 'bug catcher' installed in place of the lower aft gun turret. This featured an internal access panel to enable the retrieval of sampling filters in flight. This particular feature allowed the RB-29 to detect evidence of the use of nuclear weapons and allowed it to track any subsequent fallout cloud.

In the early 1950s the USAF would designate these aircraft the WB-29. Converted B-50As, known as WB-50s would take over from the worn out WB-29s

SB-29 Air-Sea-Rescue

The SB-29 was a natural development to help long-range rescue, with the SB-29s entering service in 1949. Each SB-29 carried the all-metal 30ft (9.1m) EDO Corporation A-3 Lifeboat, which could sustain twelve survivors for thirty days. The A-3 featured a small outboard engine that, once the A-3 had landed, was controlled and guided by the navigator to the ditched aircrew by remote control. Known as the Super Dumbo, sixteen SB-29s entered service with the USAAFs Air Rescue Service in February 1947, and were crewed by eleven personnel, including two scanning aircrew. The search was further aided by the addition of an AN/APQ-13 search radar which replaced the lower forward gun turret.

The SB-29 would provide support in the Korean War where it would gradually replace the slower SB-17s which had been struggling to keep up with the large B-29 bomber streams. On operational use the SB-29 would shadow the main bombing

SB-29 with a U.S. Navy Grumman F9F-5P from Composite Squadron VC-61 was assigned to Carrier Air Group 14 (CVG-14) aboard the aircraft Carrier *USS Boxer* (CVA-21). (US Navy)

force, before taking up station at a suitably safe point away from the bombing mission, but close enough to save lives.

During the conflict the SB-29s would save numerous lives, but after the cessation of hostilities their service life was limited and they were eventually replaced by Douglas SC-54Ds.

B-29 AEW (Airborne Early Warning)

Technology, especially radar, continued to be developed after the Second World

A starboard study of the SB-29, complete with A-3 Life Boat and AN/APQ-13 search radar. (USAF)

B-29 AEW featured an AN/APS-20C search radar as well as electronic counter measures equipment. (USAF)

D-558-2 being pushed into position for mounting to its P2B-1S launch aircraft. (NASA)

War, and the Korean War proved that jet-powered fighters were going to present new challenges. The USAF was quick to recognize the challenges and in 1951 three B-29s were modified as part of a development programme for airborne early warning (AEW) picket aircraft. The three B-29s were modified to house an AN/APS-20C search radar and electronic counter-measures equipment. The programme piqued the interests of Strategic Air Command and Air Defense Command and gave the USAF valuable experience in operating the type. This in turn lead to the design and procurement of more suitable contemporary aircraft which included Lockheed's RC-121 Warning Star.

Navy P2B-1S patrol bomber
The B-29 was far from restricted to air force use and on 14 March 1947 the USN would eventually purchase four B-29s for completing long-range maritime missions. After the first two aircraft had been suitably modified for naval use, they were redesignated as the P2B-1S. The modifications included fitting long-range fuel tanks and a picket system radar into the bomb bays.

One of the four aircraft was further modified as a mothership, known as 'Fertile Myrtle'; it was fitted with a specially designed bomb bay carrying cradle; a portion of the rear fuselage was removed. This allowed the mothership to carry and safely deploy the navy's high-speed research aircraft made by Douglas, the D-558-2 Skyrocket.

On 20 November 1953, the 'Fertile Myrtle', carried and launched the D-558-2 piloted by Scott Crossfield which would fly twice the speed of sound. The Skyrocket flights would continue until December 1956.

A further two B-29s would incorporate the experiences learned with operating the P2B-1S and modified accordingly. These would have all their defensive armament removed and would operate as anti-submarine patrol bombers, designated P2B-2S.

MX-767 'Banshee' – the B-29-based Cruise Missile Project
One of the US Air Force's Air Material Command's first post-war trials was to develop an intercontinental aircraft capable of flying a payload from the continental United States to Eurasia. At the time the Convair B-36 was still very much in development and the capacity to launch a nuclear-armed aircraft from an aircraft carrier was impractical. As such, Project MX-767, known as 'Banshee', was launched with the intention of utilizing the B-29's excellent range and turning it into a one-trip flying nuclear-armed cruise missile. For this project the aircraft involved received the designation MB-29, with 'M' standing for Missile.

Early control-equipment tests were carried out on manned B-29s which were to be guided by the wartime SHORAN (Short-Range-Navigation) automatic radio navigation system. Once the system was proved, the intention was to link the

A port view of the B50D of the 97th Bombardment Wing showing its long-range under-wing tanks and streamlined forward upper-gun turret. (US Govt)

An RB-50F of the Military Air Transport Service Air Photographic and Charting Service modified with cartographic SHORAN radar warming up its engines. (USGOV-PD)

SHORAN to the B-29's autopilot system, thus guiding the B-29 to its target. As the research progressed, the need to develop a special electromechanical computer became apparent. The computer would consider a series of factors including comparing the magnetic heading with the SHORAN signals. The system was soon deemed unreliable, and it was decided a shadowing aircraft, a DB-17 or DB-29 Drone Director, would control the MB-29, taking it as close to the target was possible, before enabling the SHORAN autopilot of the MB-29.

The SHORAN remained problematic, especially as it wasn't designed for long-distance flight and was limited by the globe's curvature and relied on line-of-sight operation. One solution was to fix two manned aircraft, known as Lighthouse airplanes with transponders to help guide the MB-29, however this had its challenges, including the possible destruction of transponder-equipped aircraft. A system involving AN / APA-44 and AN / APQ-13A radars supplying data to a CP- (XA-19) / APN-56 transponder-governing computer was eventually established.

The project continued to stagger along, with technicians struggling to make the technology work. They also had to factor in some of the B-29's more unfavourable characteristics, including engine fires, which saw the loss of one of the MB-29s in October 1948. By the end 1948 the first successful flight had taken place with training flights beginning in February 1949. There were now seven B-29s involved; two MB-29s

and five DB-29 Drone Director aeroplanes, which took over the role of the DB-17s.

After further refinements the first fully automated SHORAN-directed flight took place on 14 June 1949, armed with a simulated load and a crew of seven, in case the MB-29 erred. The flight was a success, and the experimentation group became the 550th technical squadron of guided missiles. The celebrations were short-lived and on 3 October 1949 it was recommend the 550th be stood down. The reasons were many, including the B-29's unreliability and the building up of the B-36 force which would become Strategic Air Command's (SAC) primary nuclear weapons delivery aeroplane. Another more practical point was that the system required three aircraft in the air to control the single MB-29. Not only was this expensive, but it relied on the aircraft involved not engaging enemy forces while being protected by a well-coordinated series of rolling fighter screens.

Like its predecessor, the B-50 was highly adaptable. The WB-50D was based at RAF Burtonwood, Lancashire, United Kingdom. (RuthAS)

XB-44/B-50 family

Aircraft of the B-50 family were the final expression of the Superfortress design. The B-50A was first flown on 25 June 1947. As well as featuring the upgrades made during the B-29D/XB-44 testing programme, the aircraft had an underwing capacity of 8,000lbs (3,600kg), improved avionics and strengthened landing gear. The choice of the aircraft name was merely a marketing ruse to imply the B-50A was a completely new aircraft. Remarkably the renaming worked and seventy-eight B-50As were ordered, alongside eleven TB-50 training aircraft, making the B-50 the last piston-powered bomber supplied by Boeing to the USAF.

Boeing began the YB-50C developments in 1948; this would feature a single bomb bay and larger airframe and wings. However, this project was cancelled as the B-36 was now becoming available alongside the first generation nuclear-capable jet-powered bombers. Instead, forty-five B-50Bs were ordered, which incorporated the lessons learned from their predecessors, with an increased maximum take-off weight. The B-50Bs would be converted into RB-50s which were fitted with a nine-camera pod, extra weather equipment and an increased crew. A single B-50 was modified to trial a bicycle undercarriage system before trialling a caterpillar-type undercarriage.

The final B50 was the 'D' series, of which 222 were ordered. As with previous B-50As these were capable of being refuelled in flight, but in this case using Boeing's Flying boom type. Eleven would be converted into unarmed TB-50Ds with others being converted to WB-50 standard to replace worn out WB-29s, operating between 1953 and 1955. These aeroplanes were fitted with doppler radar, atmospheric sampling equipment, to detect Soviet atomic weapons' detonation, and additional fuel tanks housed in the bomb bay.

Other variants followed, mirroring B-29-based types, but the most interesting was the KB-50J. It was converted from 112 various-series B-50s and benefitted from the fitting of two underwing General Electric J47 turbojets in prominent nacelles outside the outer engines.

A US Marine Corps North American FJ-4B of Marine Attack Squadron VMA-214 is refuelled by a KB-50J. (US Navy National Museum of Naval Aviation)

Despite being capable of flying higher, faster, and longer than the B-29 series of aircraft, the B-50 would finally be retired in the spring of 1965 as a result of metal fatigue and corrosion.

B-54

The B-54 Ultrafortress was a development of the YB-50C by Boeing who was keen to develop a main production aeroplane, the B-54A, and a reconnaissance aeroplane, the RB-54, from their work. Work started in 1947 not long after Convair's huge B-36 had made its maiden flight. The B-54 would be fitted with four Pratt & Whitney R-4360-51 Variable Discharge Turbine (VDT) engines, fitted to larger wings – 161ft (49m) – propelling a lengthened fuselage hull – 111ft (34m). This increase would see Boeing install outrigger landing gear in the first and fourth engine nacelles, with additional

The B-54 was obsolete before it left the drawing board, yet some innovations lived on. Note the tail gunner's radar, similar to that found on the early B-52s. (San Diego Air & Space Museum)

Above: When is a B-29 not a B-29? When it's a Tupolev Tu-4. This example is on display at the Central Air Force Museum, Monino, Moscow Oblast. (Alan Wilson)

Left: The KJ-1 was a domestic attempt to produce a viable AEW aircraft, but platform obsolescence brought the project to a close. (Allen Watkin)

fuel carried in two underwing pods giving the B-54 an intended range of 9,300 miles (15,000km). For defence, the B-54 was fitted with fourteen .50in guns in the turrets and for offensive operations could carry a bomb load of 36,000Ibs (16,000kg), almost double that of the original B-29. An order in May 1948 was cancelled in 1949 as the B-36s were coming into service and Boeing's first generation jet engine bomber, the B-47 Stratojet, was well on the way towards its acceptance into service.

Union of Soviet Socialist Republics

The Soviets reverse-engineered two versions of the B-29 after studying examples that landed or crashed in Soviet-held territory after being damaged in missions against Japanese targets.

Tu-70/75

The first Soviet reproduction of the B-29 by the Tupolev Design Bureau was the reverse-engineered Tu-70 airliner which first flew on 27 November 1946. The Tu-70 used salvaged B-29 outer-wing panels, engine cowlings, flaps, undercarriage and tail assembly. Featuring a wider body than the B-29, the Tu-70 used the same problematic supercharger on its Shvetsov ASh-73TK radial engines, resulting in the same problems experienced by the B-29, especially the earlier models.

Although a useful project for kick starting post-war Soviet civil airliner development, the Tu-70, and its later military cargo development the Tu-75, failed to make serial production. It did work as a useful test bed for future military transport aircraft with the Scientific-Research Institute of the Air Forces (NII VVS) between 1951 and 1954.

Tu-4 Bull

The Tu-4 (NATO reporting name Bull) first flew on 19 May 1947 after an extensive reverse-engineering programme which had seen the Tupolev Design Bureau struggle between American imperial measurements and their metric equivalents. The Tu-4 was unveiled on 3 August 1947 at the Tushino Aviation Day parade. Initially three aircraft, believed to be the three American B-29s that had landed in Soviet territory, flew over. Moments later they were joined by a fourth, leaving observers in no doubt that the Soviets had produced their own version. The Americans now realized their territories were in reach of a Soviet attack, even if Tu-4s were on a one-way trip, vulnerability had been exposed.

The basic bomber version was soon followed by a series of specialist versions, some echoing American and British use, including ELINT and ECM aircraft, a mothership for the burgeoning Soviet speed race and an escort fighter mothership. The key variants were the nuclear-capable Tu-4A, the anti-shipping Tu-4K/KS and the Tu-4R long-range reconnaissance type. A troop-carrying version, the Tu-4D, was also

'Ladybird' at Eglin Field, Fort Walton, Florida, June 1944. Lietenant Colonel Paul Tibbets and crew with Women Airforce Service Pilots (WASP) Dorothea Johnson Moorman and Dora Dougherty Strother. (USAF)

The end for many B-29s as engines and systems were harvested for valuable spares, with the remaining airframe scrapped. (San Diego Air & Space Museum)

developed. This version carried detachable underwing cargo pods for deploying with airborne troops.

People's Republic of China

The PRC received ten Tu-4s from the Soviets on 28 February 1953, which were followed by two more for navigation training in 1960. The Chinese were clearly fond of their Tu-4s, keeping them in service until 1988 and refitting their fleet with AI-20K turboprop engines between 1970 and 1973. The People's Liberation Army Air Force (PLAAF) also attempted to develop their first AEW (Airborne Early Warning) aircraft using the Tu-4, known as the KJ-1 in 1969. Despite ten years of study and development the project was cancelled in 1979 and the Tu-4 platform was declared obsolete.

National Users

Regardless of being a well-known aeroplane, the B-29 was only officially used by three air forces and two through reverse-engineered projects from interned B-29s.

United States Army Air Force (USAAF)/ United States Air Force (USAF)

The United States were the sole operators of the B-29 during the Second World War, establishing the Twentieth Air Force on 4 April 1944 to operate the new Very Heavy Bomber. Initially led by General Henry Arnold, the 20th AF would see action in the Chinese Burma India Theatre (CBI) before taking the battle to the Japanese Home Islands and fighting in the Korean War. The 20th would be stood down on 1 March 1955.

On 18 September 1947 the United Sates founded its own independent air force, and within this organization sat Strategic Air Command (SAC), founded on 21 March 1946. As part of its Order of Battle SAC was able to field B-29s and B-50s of the 2nd, 8th and 15th Air Forces should the need arise. Both versions would fly during the Korean War on a range of roles. The B-50 would also serve with the Tactical Air Command (TAC), fulfilling refuelling tasks as the KB-50 variant.

The United States Navy (USN) would also operate the four B-29s it had inherited from the USAAF.

Royal Air Force (RAF)

The RAF was loaned eighty-eight previously stored B-29As to temporarily fill its strategic-capabilities gap between the operational Avro Lincoln and the arrival of the English Electric Canberra. Known as the Washington B.1, the aeroplanes were supplied as part of the Mutual Defence Assistance Program (MDAP). The only changes to the Washington in RAF service

Three RAF B-29A Washington's in formation flight. (Royal Air Force)

were the replacement of the original long-range hyperbolic radio navigation system known as LORAN, which was replaced by the more familiar British Gee radio navigation system.

The Washington would enter service with eight Bomber Command squadrons from June 1950 until March 1954, flying from two RAF Stations: Marham and Coningsby. In addition to the Bomber Command squadrons, 192 Squadron, which fulfilled the Air Interception and Identification role or Electronic Intelligence (ELINT) role, received RB-29s. These Washingtons were tasked by Signals Command to monitor Soviet naval activity and land communications, often flying along the East–West German border. Based at RAF Watton from April 1952 until February 1958 these Washingtons flew alongside the English Electric Canberra as well as the new de Havilland Comet. Of note were 192 Squadron's Washington's which were stripped of all defensive armament.

Royal Australian Air Force (RAAF)

In 1952 two Washington B.1s were transferred from the RAF to the RAAF for the purpose of testing on behalf of the Ministry of Supply by the Aircraft Research and Development Unit. The trial included trials of weapons systems, including the UB.109T Red Rapier first generation cruise missile. Both aircraft were stripped of all defensive armament and flew until 1956. They were subsequently sold for scrap in 1957.

Soviet Air Forces (Voyenno-Vozdushnyye Sily (VVS))

The story of Russia's use of the B-29 has its roots in the early stages of the USAAF bombing campaign against the Japanese islands when damaged aircraft were unable to land at friendly sites elsewhere. The aircraft were subsequently interned with crews separated from their aircraft. For the Soviets this was a dream come true as a total of four B-29s arrived in their territories, albeit harassed by ground and air fire.

The Soviets were quick to breakdown the B-29's secrets as they had been denied the

B-29A Washington B.1 of 90th Squadron, RAF Marham, Norfolk, United Kingdom on display at the 1952 Battle of Britain show at RAF Hooton Park, Cheshire 20 September. (RuthAS)

A Chinese Tu-4 carrying underwing WuZhen-5 unmanned reconnaissance aerial vehicles (URAV), which were reverse-engineered copies of the American QM-34N 'Firebee'. (Flavio Mucia, AMB Brescia)

use of the aircraft by the Americans as part of the Lend-Lease programme. Eventually Tupolev would manage to reverse engineer the damaged aircraft, producing the Tu-4 and the Tu-70.

The Tu-70 did not enter serial production, but the Tu-4 did, with Tupolev building 847 units, some of which would enter service with the People's Liberation Army Air Force of the People's Republic of China.

The men who worked to make the B-29 atomic ready as part of Project Alberta. (Los Alamos National Laboratory)

B-29 'Enola Gay'
393rd Bombardment Squadron, Heavy, 509th Composite Group, 58th Bombardment Wing, Very Heavy
The 'Enola Gay' was named after its pilot, Colonel Paul Tibbets' mother; Tibbets was commander of the 509th Composite Group. 'Enola Gay' was one of fifteen B-29s built to Silverplate special-weapons standard for the Manhattan Nuclear Research and Development Project. On the morning of 6 August 1945 Tibbets and his crew flew to the designated target, the Japanese city of Hiroshima in the south of Japan. At 0815 local time the uranium-fuelled bomb 'Little Boy' was released, detonating 44.4 seconds later. It became the first nuclear weapon to be used offensively.

B-29 'Bockscar'
393rd Bombardment Squadron, Heavy 509th Composite Group, 58th Bombardment Wing, Very Heavy
On 9 August 1945, three days after the Hiroshima attack, 'Bockscar', another Silverplate B-29, dropped a plutonium-fuelled bomb 'Fat Man', a specially armed 'Pumpkin Bomb', on the city of Nagasaki. 'Bockscar' was named after its captain, Frederick Bock. The intended target had been the city of Korkua, home to the Imperial Japanese Army's arsenal, but due to cloud coverage the crew flew on to the secondary target of Nagasaki. At 1058 local time 'Bockscar' dropped 'Fat Man' which exploded forty-three seconds later. 'Fat Man' would be the second and final nuclear weapon used offensively.

Boeing WB-29 'Typhoon Goon'
514th Very Long-Range Weather Reconnaissance Squadron
The 514th, stationed in Guam, had an interesting and chequered history, originally forming as the 514th Bombardment Squadron, Heavy, on 19 October 1942. It was later renamed the 514th Bombardment Squadron, Heavy, on 3 May 1944 and once more as the 514th Bombardment Squadron, Very Heavy, on 23 May 1945. After the war the 514th flew on until it was stood down on 7 March 1946. On 16 September 1947 it was reformed as the 514th Reconnaissance Squadron, Very Long Range, Weather, to which 'Typhoon Goon' belonged. She was tasked with weather-related reconnaissance, including twenty-five typhoon tracking missions. 'Typhoon Goon' was finally retired in December 1950.

Camouflage & Markings 47

Washington B.I
Royal Air Force, Bomber Command
In Royal Air Force (RAF) service the B-29 was known as the Washington B.I which filled a gap in the RAF's strategic capabilities until the English Electric Canberra was in squadron service. The eighty-seven B-29As were loaned to the RAF as part of the Mutual Defence Assistance Program in February 1950. Eventually the B-29s were returned to the United Sates as the Canberra became available. The last B-29s were used until 1958 by 192nd Squadron, RAF Watton, Norfolk, for Electronic Intelligence operations after which they were relegated as ground targets.

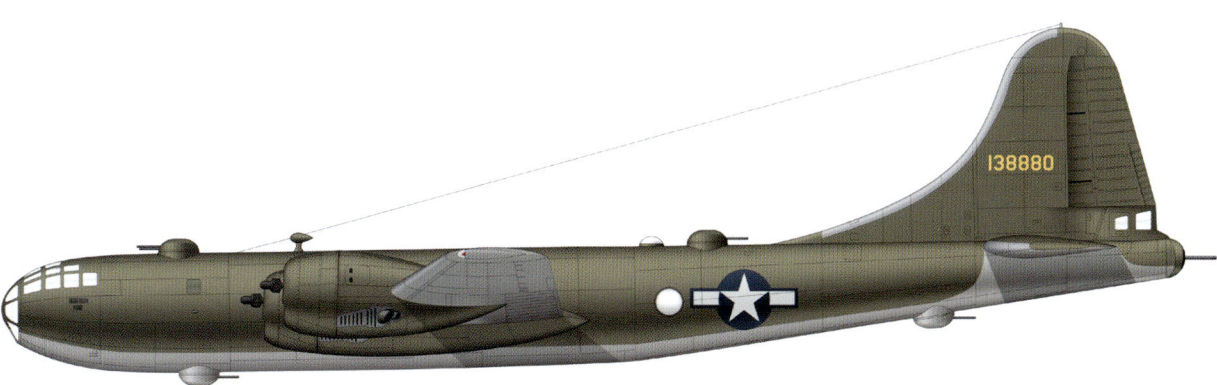

YB-29
An experimental B-29
A YB-29 in a factory-fresh Olive Drab over Neutral Gray scheme and featuring the three-blade propeller which was replaced with the more efficient four-blade version on serial production aircraft. Of interest is the bare metal leading edges of the wings, which were a result of initial issues with the logistics. This meant early aircraft were missing their rubber de-icing boots. This, and other supply issues, would be resolved by Major General Bennett Meyers in what was to be called the Battle of Kansas.

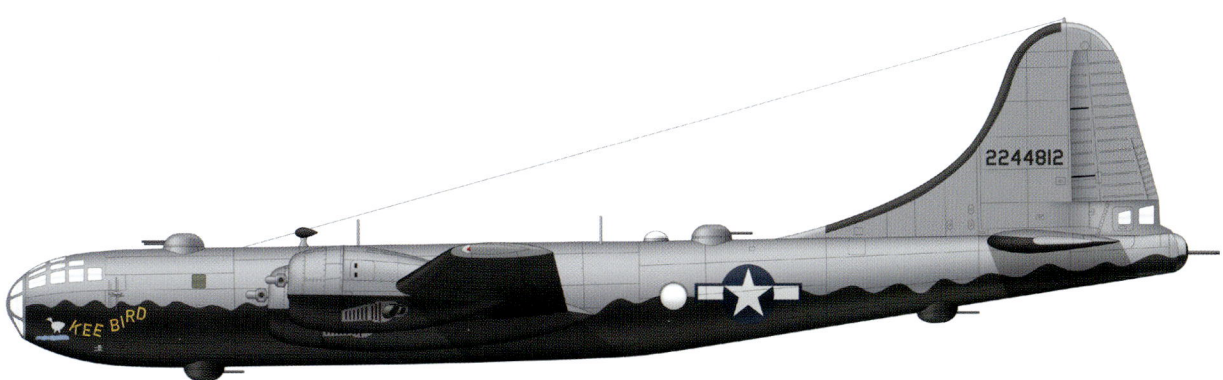

B-29 'Kee Bird'
46th Reconnaissance Squadron
The 'Kee Bird' was flown by the 46th Reconnaissance Squadron, based at Ladd Field, Alaska Territory, 'Kee Bird' was part of Project Nanook which conducted long-range aerial reconnaissance over the Arctic to assess the Soviet threat. On 21 February 1947 'Kee Bird' was forced to make an emergency landing on a lake in Greenland because of pilot disorientation. The crew were successfully rescued. In 1995 the 'Kee Bird' was located by a team led by Darryl Greenamyer and prepared for flight. Unfortunately, an onboard fire during preparations for flight destroyed the aircraft, with the wreckage remaining atop the frozen lake.

Tupolev Tu-4 'Bull'
Soviet Air Force
The Tupolev Tu-4 'Bull' surprised Western observers when it appeared on 3 August 1947 at the Tushino Aviation Day Parade. The Soviets had done a good job of reverse-engineering interned B-29s; though they had also incorporated the aeroplane's many foibles, including engine fires. The Tu-4 would be shared with the People's Liberation Army Air Force and would produce a series of variants including a Tu-4 AWACS.

KB-29 P Tanker Aircraft
509th Air Refuelling Squadron, Strategic Air Command, United States Air Force
The KB-29 P Tanker Aircraft was the first to use Boeing's rigid flying-boom system and entered service with the 509th in 1952 replacing the KB-29M tanker, which used hoses to refuel aircraft. The new rigid flying-boom system was visually controlled by the operator peering out of a domed Plexiglas section which replaced the rear armament. 483397, shown here, as she appeared while at RAF Lakenheath, Suffolk, United Kingdom in 1954. That year the 509th would convert to the short-lived KC-97 Tankers.

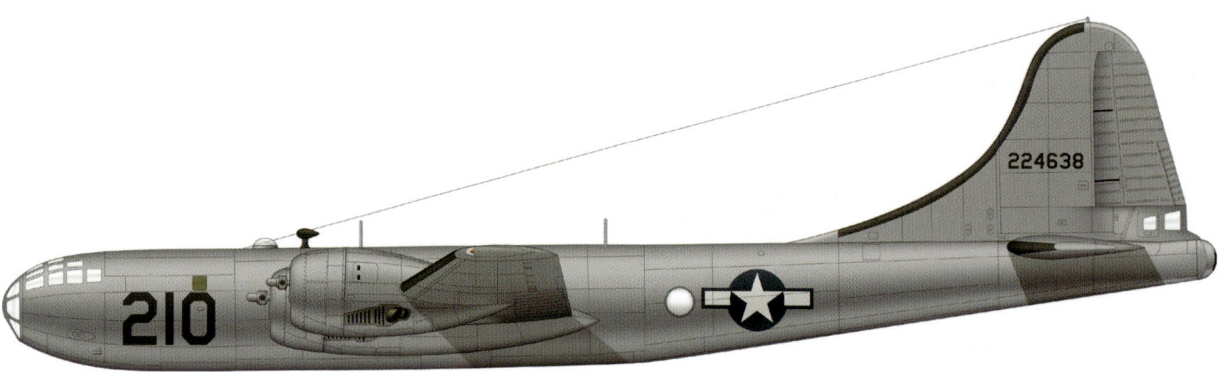

TB-29
Army Air Training Command Transitioning Training School
This aeroplane filled an important role in preparing the next generation of aircrews for operations in the B-29 and was known as the TB-29. It belonged to the Army Air Training Command Transitioning Training School based at Maxwell Field, Alabama, United States. The TB-29s would carry four three-man teams of new commanders, pilots and flight engineers who would receive their training from one pilot instructor and one flight engineer instructor over a five-week period before being released for squadron service.

B-29 '20th Century Unlimited'
45th Bomb Squadron, 40th Bombardment Group, 58th Bombardment Wing, Very Heavy
B-29 '20th Century Unlimited' belonged to the 45th Bomb Squadron, 40th Bombardment Group, 58th Bombardment Wing, Very Heavy, which was based at Kharagpur, India. '20th Century Unlimited' flew from several bases in the China-Burma-India Theatre (CBI) including Chakulia, India, and the advanced China Base at Hsinching Airfield, as part of Operation Matterhorn. This was the name given to operations from India and China against Imperial Japanese targets in the South East Asia. '20th Century Unlimited' would be destroyed on 29 July 1944 after an explosion at West Field, Tinian, Mariana Islands.

B-29 'Eddie Allen'
45th Bomb Squadron, 40th Bomb Group, 58th Bombardment Wing, Very Heavy
B-29 'Eddie Allen' was named in honour of the well-known and extremely capable test pilot Edmund Allen. Allen's systematic approach to the art of flying ensured the safety of many who would fly the new generation multi-engine aircraft. Allen was killed while testing the first XB-29 on 21 September 1942. The aircraft was paid for by donations from the employees of Boeing Wichita and gifted to the USAAF. It completed twenty-four missions before being damaged beyond repair. 'Eddie Allen' was part of 45th Bomb Squadron, 40th Bomb Group, 58th Bombardment Wing, Very Heavy.

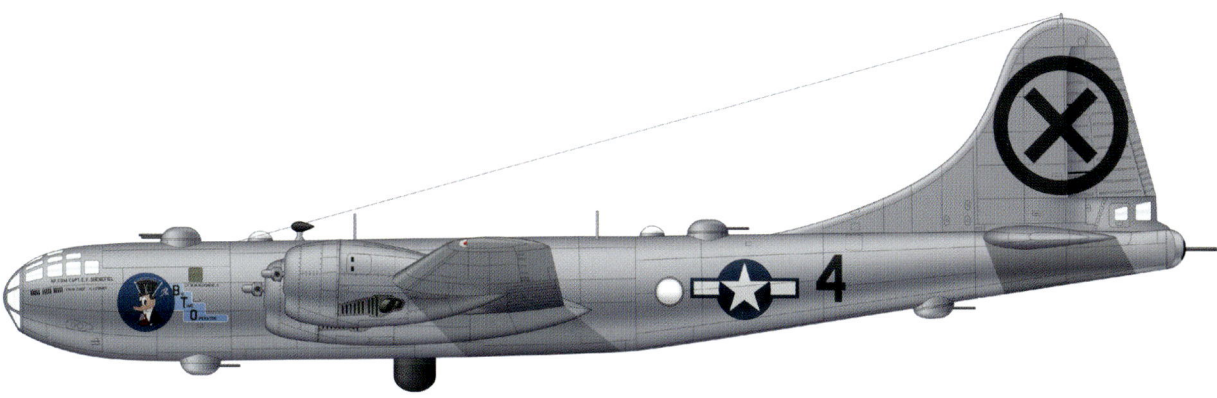

B-29 'Big Time Operator'
1st Bomb Squadron, Very Heavy, 9th Bomb Group, 313th Bomb Wing
B-29 'Big Time Operator' served with 1st Bomb Squadron, Very Heavy, 9th Bomb Group, 313th Bomb Wing from 17 October 1944. 'Big Time Operator' would complete a total of forty-six combat missions over Imperial Japanese territory. After the war she returned to the United States and in 1950 was stricken from the inventory. She was subsequently transferred to the US Navy as one of thirty-six B-29s used as ground targets at China Lake Naval Weapons Station, California.

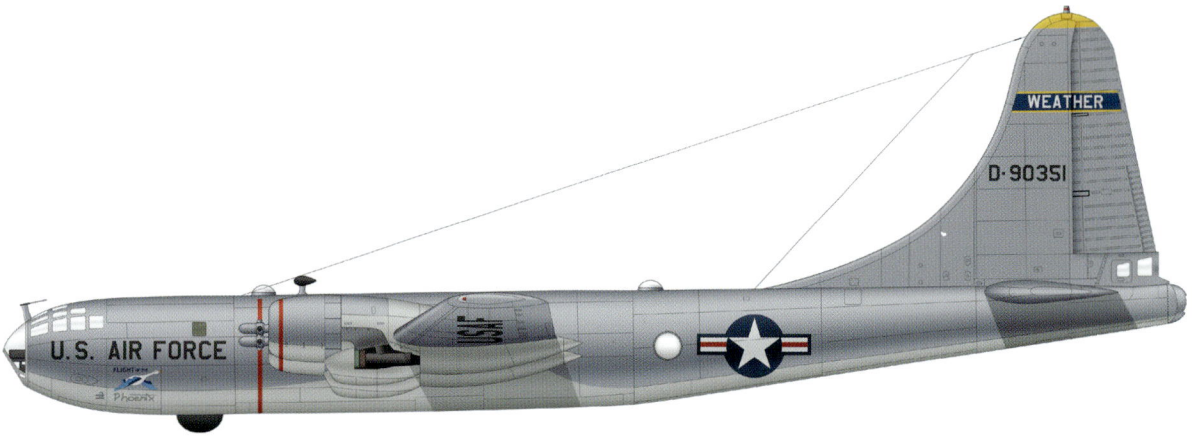

WB-50D 'Flight of the Phoenix'
53rd Weather Reconnaissance Squadron, USAF
Initially finished as a B-50D before conversion to a WB-50D, 'Flight of the Phoenix' served as a weather reconnaissance aircraft with the 53rd Weather Reconnaissance Squadron based at RAF Burtonwood, Lancashire from 1953. The WB-50D could fly higher and faster and longer than the worn-out WB-29s it replaced. It monitored the weather, with some aircraft carrying out highly classified atmospheric sampling missions and was used to detect Soviet detonations of atomic weapons. 'Flight of the Phoenix' would move to the Military Aircraft Storage and Disposition Center (MASDC) on 7 March 1965 before being released as a heritage airframe for museum use on 14 March 1972.

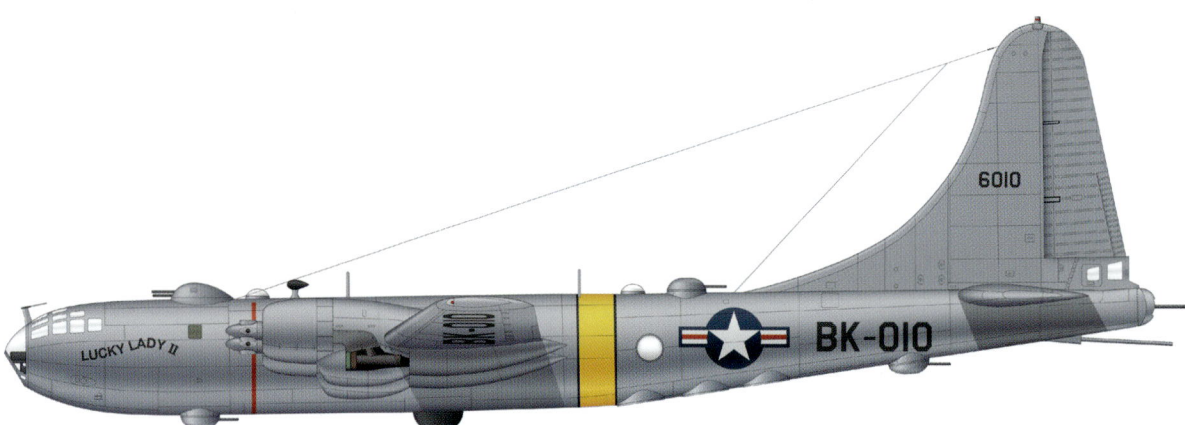

B-50A 'Lucky Lady II'
43rd Bombardment Group
B-50A 'Lucky Lady II' holds a unique place in aviation history: the first aircraft to circle the globe nonstop in 1949. In a journey taking ninety-four hours and one minute 'Lucky Lady II' made the journey between 26 February and 2 March 1949, covering 23,452 miles (37,742km). The journey started and ended at Carswell Air Force Base, Fort Worth, Texas and was refuelled four times by KB-29Ms tankers.

B-29 'Sentimental Journey'
330th Bomb Group, 458th Bombardment Squadron
B-29 'Sentimental Journey' was received by its crew late in the war, on 6 June 1945, before heading out to the Marianas ten days later. As part of 330th Bomb Group and assigned to the 458th Bombardment Squadron, 'Sentimental Journey' would be based at North Field, Guam, where she would complete thirty missions before the war's end. In March 1954 'Sentimental Journey' was renamed 'Dopey' and assigned to 4713th Radar Evaluation Squadron at Griffiss Air Force Base, New York, flying radar defence evaluation flights until retirement in June 1959.

B-29 'Three Feathers'
883rd Bomb Squadron, 500th Bomb Group, 73rd Bomb Wing
Another B-29 issued in 1945 was 'Three Feathers' which was delivered to the USAAF on 5 May. 'Three Feathers' joined 883rd Bomb Squadron, 500th Bomb Group, 73rd Bomb Wing based at Iseley Field, Saipan. After the war the aircraft joined the 581st Air Resupply Group at Kadena Air Base, Okinawa where she stayed until March 1956. Therafter she was transferred to the US Navy for use as a ground target at China Lake Naval Weapons Station, California.

B-29 'Fifi'
Commemorative Air Force
B-29 'Fifi' holds a unique place in B-29 history as being only one of two still airworthy today, the other being 'Doc'. Built in 1945 'Fifi' was initially converted to work as TB-29A where she served as an administrative aircraft. After a period of operational duty 'Fifi' was placed into storage before returning to duty in 1953. In 1958 she transferred to the US Navy for use as a ground target at China Lake Naval Weapons Station, California. She was rescued by the Confederate Air Force, now known as the Commemorative Air Force and taken back to Harlingen, Texas on 3 August 1971 for restoration. It was in late in 1974 that she was christened 'Fifi'.

B-29 'Hollywood Commando'
677th Bombardment Squadron, 444th Bombardment Group, 58th Bombardment Wing
B-29 'Hollywood Commando' belonged to 677th Bombardment Squadron, 444th Bombardment Group, 58th Bombardment Wing which initially used Charra Airfield in India as its base in the CBI Theatre. From Charra the 677th would use airfields in China, such as Kwanghan Airfield, to stage attacks against Imperial Japanese positions. Like many in-theatre B-29 groups, the 444th moved to the Marianas, with Tinian becoming the home base. 'Hollywood Commando' would be lost on a mission over Tokyo on 25 May 1945 with all crew missing in action.

B-29 'Pride of the Yankees'
882nd Squadron, 500th Bomb Group, 73rd Bomb Wing
B-29 'Pride of the Yankees' flew with the 882nd Squadron, 500th Bomb Group, 73rd Bomb Wing, which arrived at Isely Field, Saipan during October 1944. 'Pride of the Yankees' would fly its first mission on 24 November 1944. On 9 March 1945 she led the first Allied fire-bomb raid over Tokyo. That same month 'Pride of the Yankees' would loose an engine after being hit by anti-aircraft fire which seized the port inboard engine. Its propeller promptly sheared off and slammed into the propeller of the outboard engine. The pilot was able to feather the damaged propeller and limp 700 miles (1,127km) to Iwo Jima for an emergency landing. 'Pride of the Yankees' completed a total of thirty-seven missions, and eighteen engines changes before her last mission on 9 July 1945.

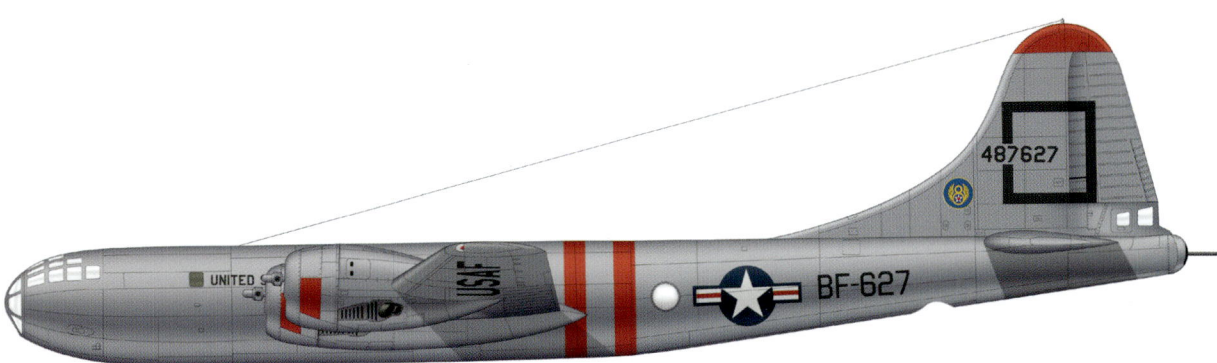

TB-29
This TB-29 led a very short, and for a B-29, unremarkable life. Built in 1944 it was converted to TB-29 standard and taken on as a crew-training airframe before being stored at China Lake California, United States. In 1956 it was released from store and sent to Philips Army Airfield, Aberdeen Proving Grounds, Maryland, where it was used as a ground target. It was recovered and restored in 1995 and is now on show at Barksdale Global Power Museum, Louisiana.

B-29 'The Great Artiste'
393rd Bomb Squadron, 509th Composite Group, 58th Bombardment Wing, Very Heavy
B-29 'The Great Artiste' is a 393rd Bomb Squadron, 509th Composite Group, 58th Bombardment Wing, Very Heavy, Silverplate B-29. 'The Great Artiste' entered service on 20 April 1945 and arrived at Tinian on 22 June 1945. The aircraft would fly twelve combat missions against targets on the Japanese Home Islands using the 'Pumpkin Bomb' on some. On 6 August 1945 it formed part of the Hiroshima bombing mission where it was used as the blast-measurement instrumentation aircraft. It had been intended to carry the Nagasaki bomb but the mission had been brought forward by two days and the instrumentation had yet to be removed. As a result 'The Great Artiste' accompanied 'Bockscar', once again as the blast-measurement instrumentation aircraft. After the war 'The Great Artiste' remained with the 509th until scrapped in September 1949.

B-29 'Straight Flush'
393rd Bomb Squadron, 509th Composite Group, 58th Bombardment Wing, Very Heavy
Another 393rd Bomb Squadron B-29, 'Straight Flush' was received by the USAAF on 2 April 1945 and flown by Captain Claude Eatherly, arriving at Tinian on 13 June. 'Straight Flush' would go on to fly six combat missions. It would later act as weather reconnaissance aircraft for the Hiroshima raid before returning to Roswell Army Airfield, New Mexico, with the rest of the 509th. In 1950 'Straight Flush' was converted to TB-29 standard serving with the 2nd Radar Calibration Squadron, Elmendorf Air Force Base, Alaska, April 1953 and the 5025th Maintenance Group, Elmendorf AFB in August 1953. 'Straight Flush' was scrapped in July 1954.

B-29 'Victor 4'
509th Composite Group, 58th Bombardment Wing, Very Heavy
'Victor 4' was another unnamed B-29, serving with the 509th Composite Group, 58th Bombardment Wing, Very Heavy. There's very little information on this particular B-29 and, like 'T-Square 54' it's fair to assume she was used as a rotational aircraft. The lack of gunners' blisters on the fuselage identifies her as one of sixty-five Silversplate B-29s built between 1944 and 1947. Of these, twenty-nine were assigned to the 509th. Note 'Victor 4' carries the original forward-pointing arrow in a circular tail marking of the 509th.

B-29A 294106
This exceptionally clean B-29A 294106 would have shone in the sun; of note is its lack of de-icing boots along it leading edges. This is one of 1,119 B-29As built, with this particular aircraft built at the Renton Works, Washington State, United States. Sadly, little information exists regarding this aircraft but its lack of markings gives the reader the opportunity to enjoy the B-29's simplicity of aerodynamic form, which belied its remarkable capabilities.

Modelling the Boeing B-29

The B-29 remains an extremely popular subject with modellers and is well served by manufacturers who have produced a wonderful range of kits in all scales over the years. All kits have their merits with great potential to add multimedia detailing and conversion parts, as well as changing markings, this helps the modeller create a very personal build of this iconic aircraft. Given the range of scales the kits can also be incorporated into both small vignettes and large-scale dioramas with other genres of model making, allowing the modeller to introduce a range of ground-support vehicles and scratch-built buildings. As new models of the B-29 are always being produced this list is purely contemporaneous and features manufactures that are trading at the time of writing. For those wishing to build the more iconic vintage construction kits, from Airfix for example, there are often opportunities to purchase these from a range of sources.

Model Kits

Due to its size the B-29 is restricted to the 1/72 and 1/48 plastic kits, with Revell/Monogram still leading with its 1/48 behemoth offering. This evergreen plastic model kit first appeared in 1977 as part of monogram's 1/48 scale multi-engine bomber range, alongside the B-17G and B-24J. Now available as a Revell kit (Nr. 03850), it comes complete with photoetch and masks for the intricately glazed nose section. Also included are markings for three separate aircraft operating in the Second World War. The kits feature a fully detailed interior along with a series of figures. As to be expected with a kit of this vintage, the B-29 is very much of its age with exposed moulding sink holes and ejector marks, although not beyond the skills of the average modeller to rectify. The panel lines are raised, the style of moulding in the 1970s, but this does not detract from the overall appearance of the kit. The kit also contains the spares to create a Silverplate conversion. This simple conversation is not beyond the skills of the average modeller and images contained in this book will help with positioning blanking covers.

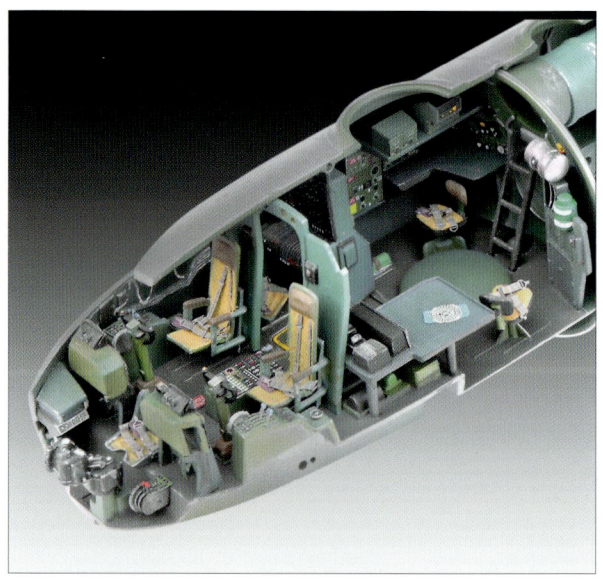

Revell's upgrade of the venerable Monogram kit delivers the modeller a suitable challenge and an opportunity for some B-29-themed vignettes.

In the 1/72 fine scale range of kits Academy's B-29 has several versions available to make, the B-29A (Nr. 12517) and the Silverplate version (Nr. 12528). First released in 1991 by Academy/Minicraft, these B-29s have gone on to be re-boxed by Modelist as the Tupolev Tu-4 (Nr. 7214) and Doyusta (Nr. 40069). Like its larger cousin these kits feature fine interior detailing while benefiting from more contemporary moulding, giving fine panel lines and sharper detail. In kit Nr. 12517 the front upper gun turret is the later four-gun type and there are also parts to make the KB-29P rigid flying boom system, giving the modeller the opportunity to create an extra version of the B-29.

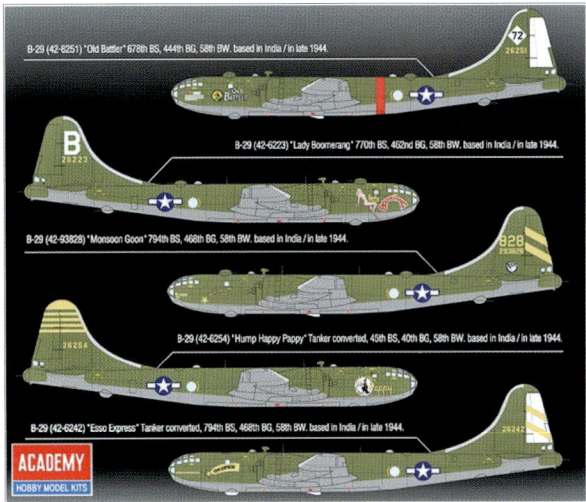

Academy's B-29 kits are among the most beautifully presented in the world, with some wonderful schemes and are packed with opportunities to develop your aero-modelling skills.

For the 1/144 micro scale or space-starved modeller there are three B-29s available from AWM (Nr. 40029), Minicraft (Nr. 14609) and Fujimi (Nr. 14428). Of the three Minicraft provides the modeller with a break from wartime service B-29s and includes marking for Korean War and RAF B-29s. It also provides an interesting addition in the bladeless propeller hub which simulates a B-29 in flight. AWM provides the modeller with a Silverplate version of the B-29 with markings for the 'Enola Gay'. The Fujimi kit features decals for wartime and Korean War versions as well as the Pumpkin Bomb and the KB-29P rigid flying boom system. Interior details are understandably muted, and Airfield Accessories offer a handy white metal cockpit section in 1/144 (Nr. 114.17) to lend weight to the finished model. While this is marketed as an Academy fit, it will fit Minicraft's B-29 which is a re-box of the 1994 Academy kit giving it some interior detailing. The Minicraft kit which is a re-boxing of the original Crown kit released in 1976 is now showing its age, with exterior details muted; it does however feature some engraved panel line, but delivers good value for money. The Fujimi kit, as you would expect, is well designed, featuring a cockpit and bomb-bay. Like the Minicraft kit, the Fujimi kit features engraved panel lines which seem sharper than those found on the Minicraft kit.

For those modellers who like to work in even smaller scales Atlantis have produced a wonderful 1/200 (Nr. H208) B-29A, which is supplied with the markings for separate aircraft, including 'FiFi', one of the last airworthy B-29s. The kit is of low part count and, as can be expected at this scale, is bare on interior details. It comes with the clear Atlantis stand which has space for the circular Boeing B-29 decal. This kit is a great representation of the B-29 in flight and would sit nicely on any modeller's shelf.

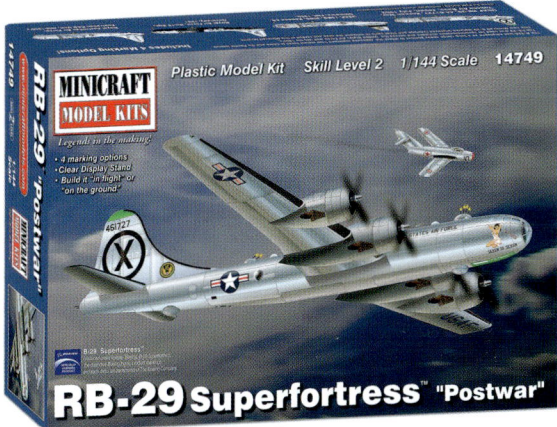

Minicraft and Fujimi continue to excel in giving the modeller great kits in 1/144.

The box art of the Atlantis B-29 has an old-school charm that delivers a kit which is easy and enjoyable build.

To join Atlantis, Pit-Road have produced a 1/700 scale box set (Nr. SPS08) entitled WWII United States 20th Air Force Mariana Islands Base. The kit features six B-29s as well as P-38, P-40, P-47 and P-51 models and a few airfield buildings. This sits alongside the Battle of Japan kit (Nr. S37SP) which features B-29s and a selection of Imperial Japanese aircraft, including the Nakajima J1N Gekko night fighter.

For detailing there is a host of photoetch from detailing doyens Eduard in 1/48 for the Revell/Monogram kits, including colour interior pieces (Nr. 49616) and undercarriage boxings (Nr. 48743). Ukrainian firm

 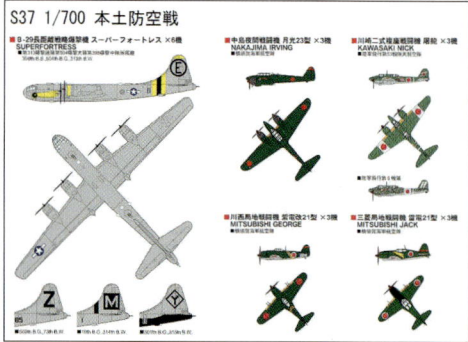

The new masters of miniature? Pit-Road more than deliver with their unique scale kits, which are aimed at the 1/700 maritime modeller, and promise some great diorama opportunities.

Metallic Details have produced a series of masks (Nr. MDM4810) alongside resin and 3-D printed parts, including the Nr. 48114 late-propeller set in 1/48 and for the Academy 1/72 kits. The Academy kits are also treated to a set of beautifully finished white metal landing gear by Scale Aircraft Conversions (Nr. 72013).

Eduard continue to innovate using resin and brass undercarriage sets and coloured etch for the Revell/Monogram B-29 kits.

Metallic Details upgrade kits for Academy's 1/72 B-29s are exquisite in their detailing.

Modelling the Boeing B-29

For decals British rising star Kits World, have produced a wide range of Second World War and Korean War decals in 1/48, 1/72 and 1/144. Kits World decals are consistently sharp, handle softening and conforming agents well with colour profiles nicely in register. They're joined by Canadian company Iliad Designs and American company Warbird Design who provide B-29 decals in 1/48 and 1/72 scales.

As with all models of tricycle aircraft the most important detail is to add weight under the B-29s cockpit flooring where possible to prevent your finished work from becoming a tail sitter.

Kits World decals are well researched and sharp, available in 1/48, 1/72 and 1/144, and provide the modeller with multiple choices to enable the growth of their B-29 fleet.

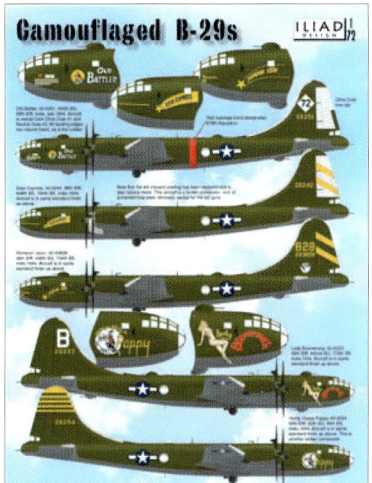

The details of Warbird Design's nose art decals in 1/48 and 1/72 are of exceptional quality and a tribute to both the original artists and the aircraft.

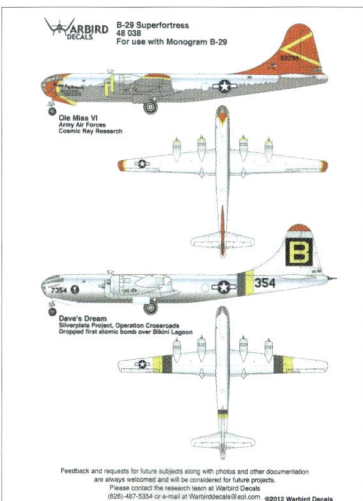

Iliad Designs have produced a set of decals for early-camouflaged B-29s in 1/48 and 1/72, which feature well-balanced yellow details for any CBI-based Superfortress.

B-29 Silverplate 'Enola Gay', 393rd Bombardment Squadron, Heavy, 509th Composite Group, North Field, Northern Mariana Islands, 6 August 1945
Monogram/Revell 1/48 B-29
Modelled by Colin Higton

This re-issue kit by Revell was originally made by Monogram and comes with some excellent photoetch, brass, and printed parts. The main thing you notice is the sheer size of the parts; the fuselage is over two-feet long, and the wingspan is almost three feet. However, it is everything you expect of a 1970s kit. It features raised panel lines and thick mouldings that need lots of adjustment to make it fit together. Revell have decided not to offer the 'Enola Gay' as one of the finish options in this kit so the markings are printed.

Sadly, most of the details in the cockpit are lost as a result of the thickness of the greenhouse canopy. The wings came second in the build process and were bolted and glued into place. This was a good opportunity to remove a lot of the original raised panel lines and to scribe replacements into the surfaces. Unsurprisingly, this kit needs a considerable amount of nose weight; several coins were glued into the lower turret position, with more hot-glued into the bomb bay. The 'Enola Gay' didn't have turrets, so these had to be carefully removed using the kit's blanks to cover the exposed apertures. Overall, the kit went together well, with the use of plasticard to assist the fit.

To assist with painting the kit is supplied with pre-cut masks which are excellent, and are applied before priming the gloss black primer, which is followed by a coat of Airframe Aluminium, which gives a high shine but very uniform finish. Post-it notes were used to mask off various panels before a range of other colours were laid down, including matt and semi-matt Aluminium, Magnesium, Chrome and black chrome to create some variety in the panels. Before applying the home-made decals the engine nacelles were fixed in place, (another couple of coins were added behind each for extra weight).

While it would be nice to have better moulds and engraved panel lines there is something to be said about crafting a model from these old kits. This one is undoubtedly magnificent.

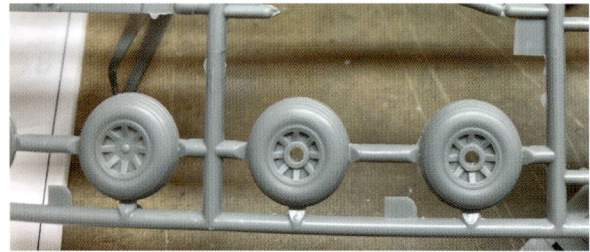

Modelling the Boeing B-29 63

Modelling the Boeing B-29 65

Modelling the Boeing B-29 67

B-29 'Bockscar' 393rd Bombardment Squadron, Heavy, 509th Composite Group, 58th Bombardment Wing, Very Heavy, 9th August 1945
Academy 1/72 B-29
Modelled by Brian Richardson

This is the Academy 1/72 B-29A Superfortress fifty-year anniversary kit released in 2018. It has new decals for 'Enola Gay' and 'Bockscar'. The kit was first tooled in 1991 and has been re-released many times over the years with new parts and decals, these include the tanker version and the B-50. A Russian company has modelled the Academy kit as the Tupolev Tu-4.

The tanker parts are still on the sprues as are the guns and turrets, so other versions could be built from this kit, just requiring replacement aftermarket decals. Overall, the kit goes together well, has very fine recessed panel lines and is straight forward.

The flight deck is well done with enough details, including decals for the pilot's instruments and engineer's console, although not much of this can be seen once the fuselage is closed up; the same applies to the waist- and tail-gunners' stations, but they are there. Separate bomb-bay doors allow both bays and tunnel to be modelled and both have adequate detail.

This kit is worth getting just for the cartography decals alone; the printing is first class. The only issues with the build were the rather vague instructions and the location of the bomb bay and undercarriage-door hydraulic arms (C24 and C44) that have poor location points. The two nose wheels also have rather nasty ejection pin marks on the tyres that will be difficult to remove. Here they have been replaced with the superior Aero Line #AL7047 resin set.

The nose-wheel doors could also do with some hinges and as there are no location points at all, these were drilled and pinned with thin wire to at least give them some strength. The kit's exhaust stubs are quite simple and a bit undersized and were replaced with the Metallic Details set that includes new engines and etch wheel wells. This set can be quite expensive (it cost more than the kit) but the result was worth it.

There's also a fair bit of surgery required to fit the resin exhaust housings into the engine mounts. The brass photoetch vented covers look much better than the kit parts as the vents are only supplied in the kit as decals. After priming, the model was given a polish and a few spots were filled, sanded and primed again. This is essential as the Alclad and SMS acrylic lacquer metallics are very unforgiving and show up every little imperfection, even after the first coats of Chrome went down a few more niggles were uncovered and had to be addressed. Various panels were treated with SMS Aluminium and Steel and Polished Aluminium as per war-time photos. Wheel hubs are aluminium and the tyres were painted with Tamiya XF-69 Nato Black. The hubs were then treated with Tamiya Dark Brown panel accent wash. The treads were dusted with some AK weathering powder and wiped over to remove any excess.

An overall coat of SMS Super Clear sealed the paint and decals. A final polish with a micro fibre cloth helps remove any over spray and restores that high-gloss finish. Clumsy handling resulted in damage to the seventy-seven decals under the nose being damaged and they aren't easy to replace as they're specific to this aircraft. However, an image of a post-war 'Bockscar' didn't show them, so they have been left off.

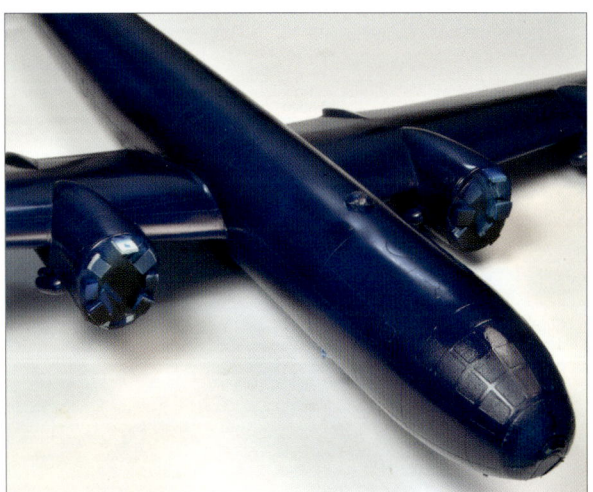

Modelling the Boeing B-29

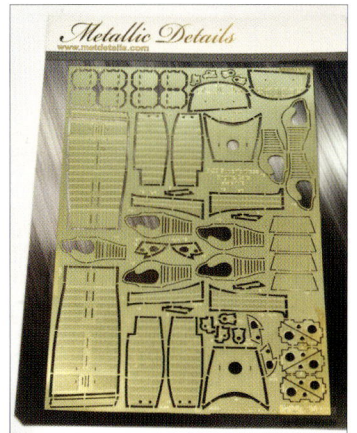

BOCKSCAR
77
NO SMOKING WITHIN
100FT.

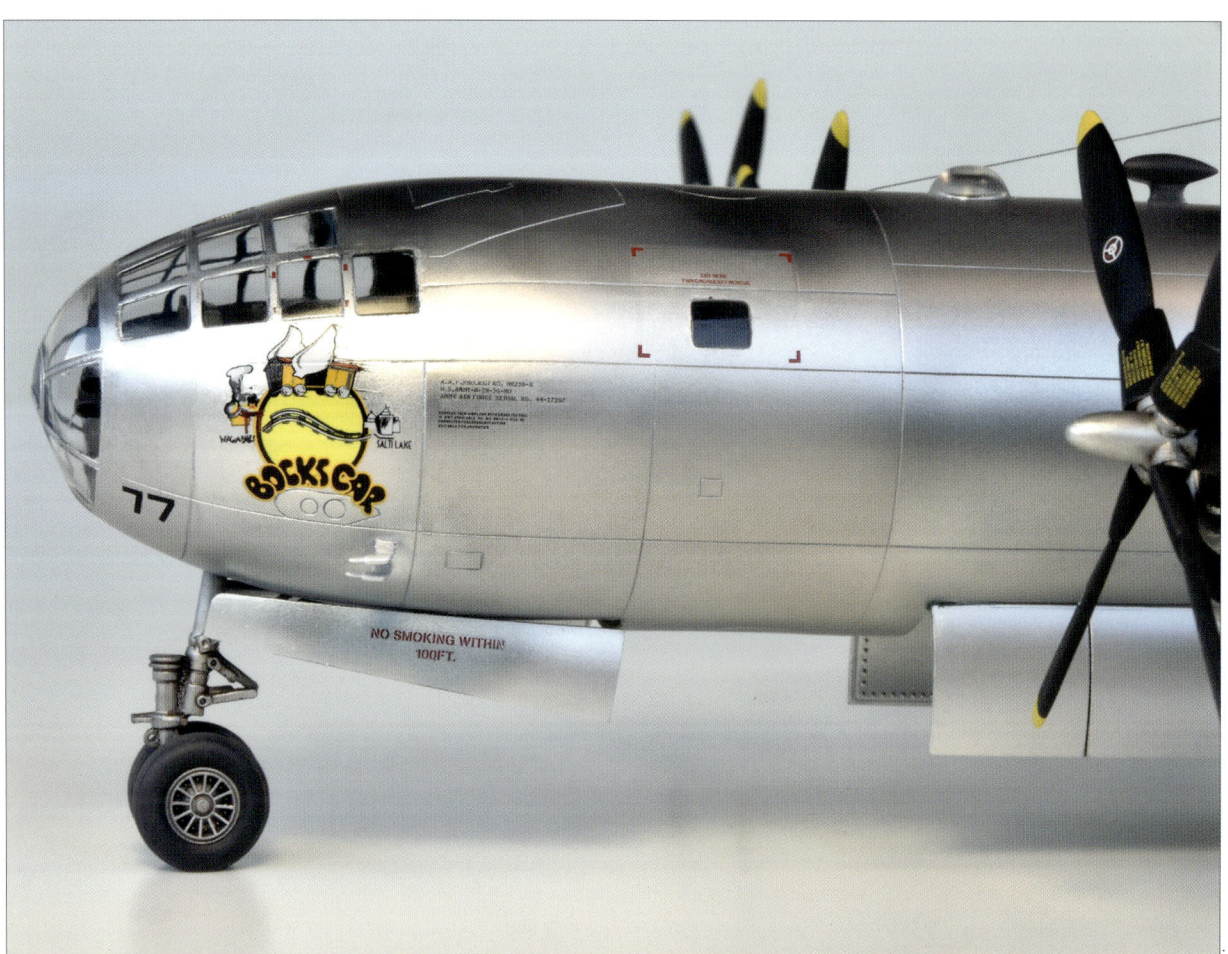

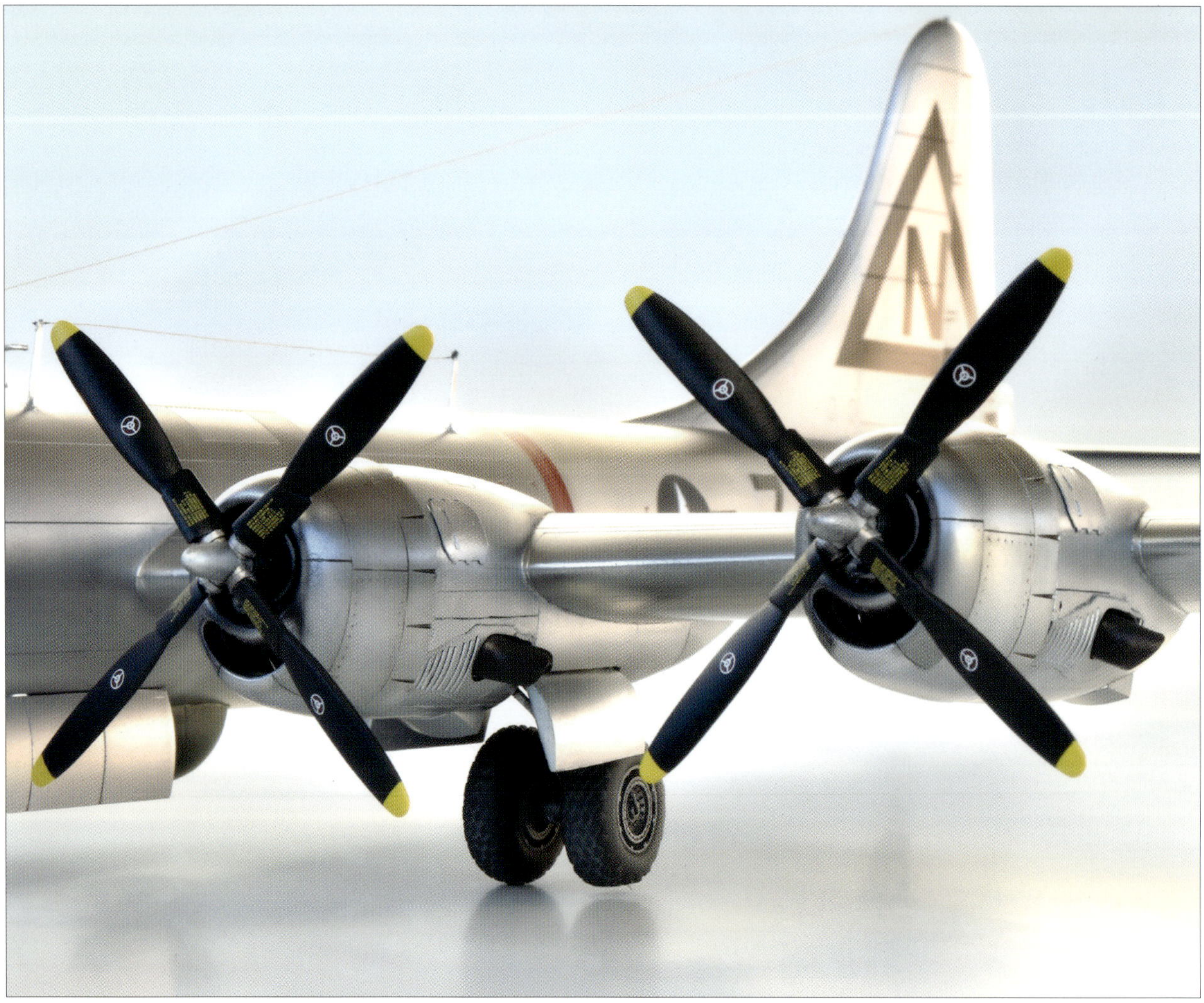

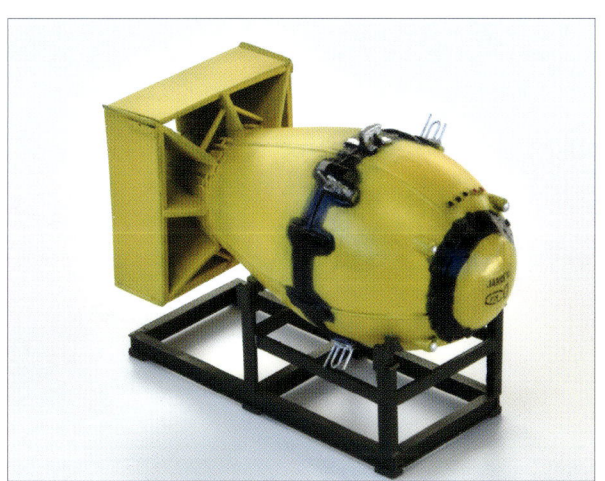
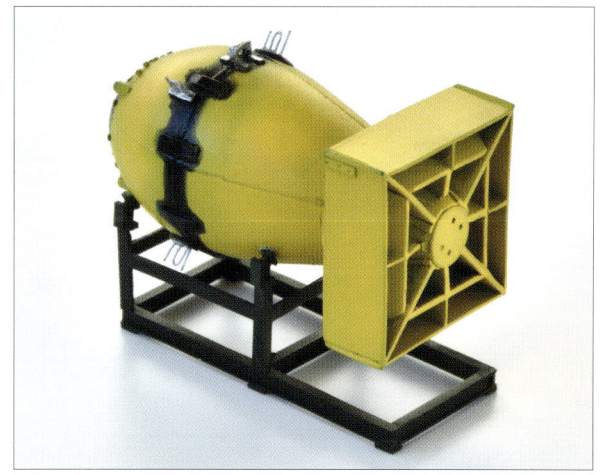

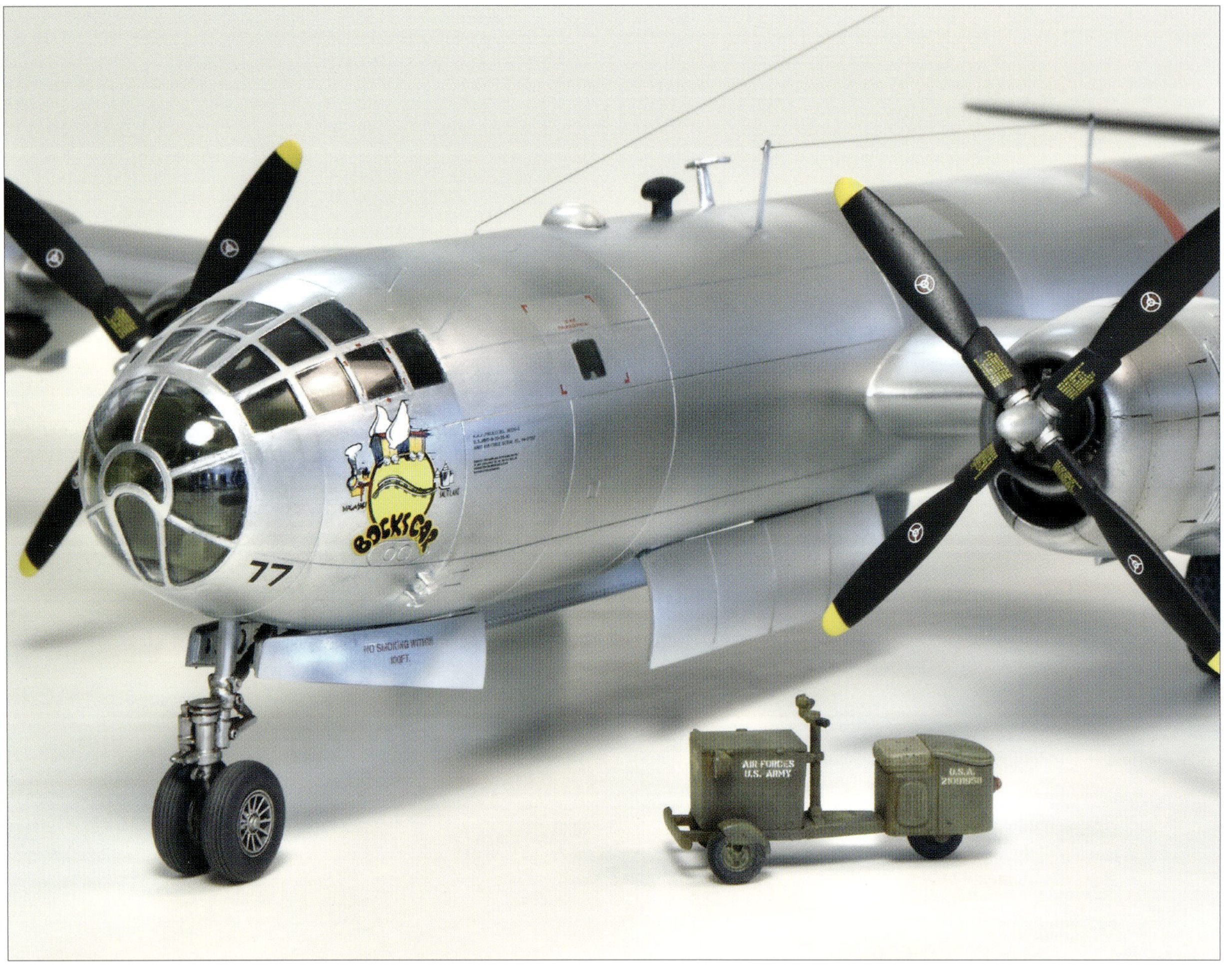

74 BOEING B-29

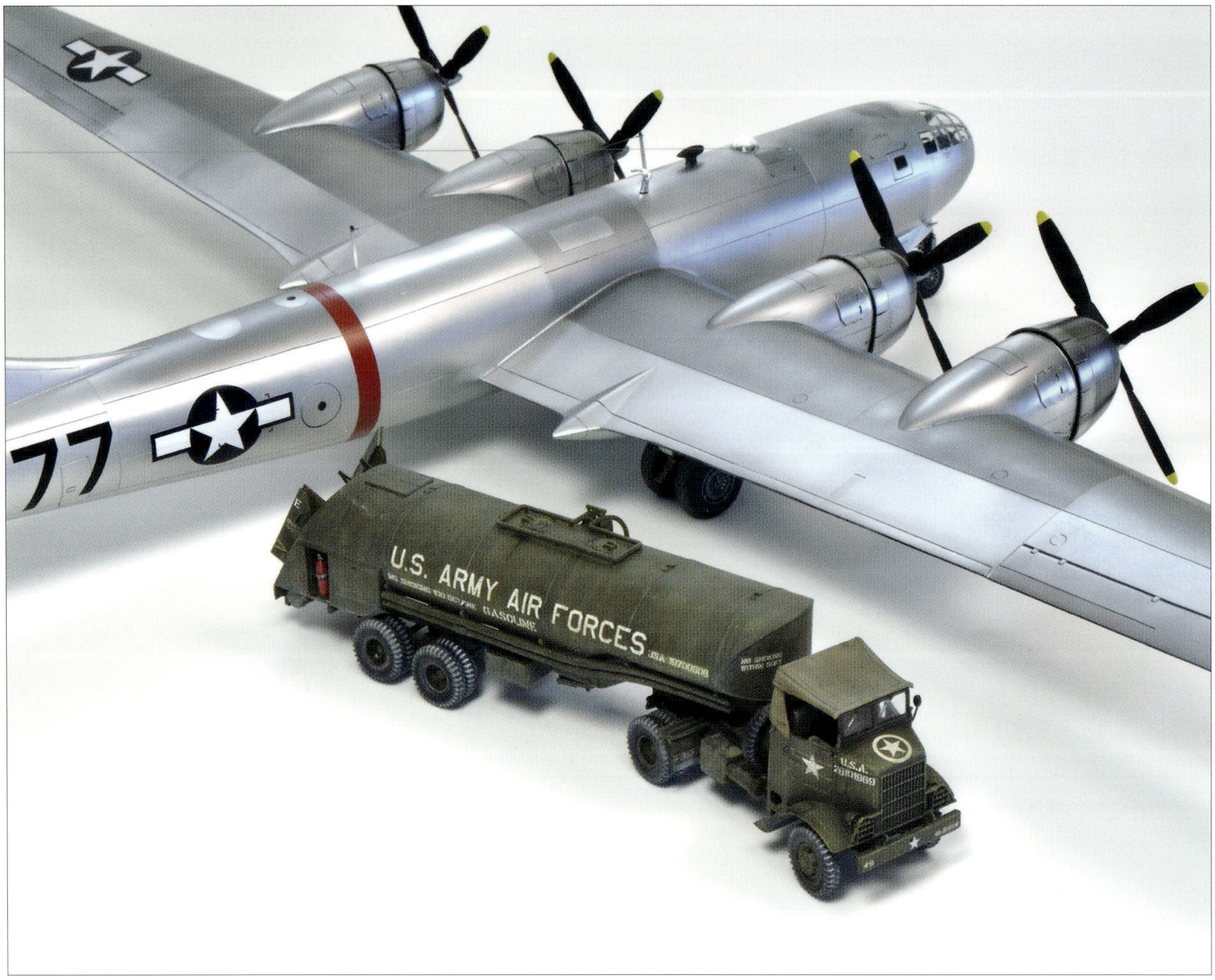

Modelling the Boeing B-29 77

B-29 'Monsoon Goon', initially assigned to 794th Squadron, 468th Bombardment Group, 58th Bomb Wing, 20th Air Force, November 1943. Later assigned to 514th Very Long-Range Weather Reconnaissance Squadron, Heavy, May 1944
Academy 1/72 B-29
Modelled by Brian Richardson

This Academy kit, 12517 was re-boxed in 2015 with new decals by Cartograph for five aircraft, three with turrets and two converted into tankers. The tankers were required to carry fuel, spare engines, and parts to forward bases in India and China from Burma. All these carry Olive Drab over Neutral Grey schemes.

'Monsoon Goon' was built nearly out of the box with new grooved wheels by Plus Model PLUS-AL7048 and MASTER .50cal gun barrels AM-72-125. Some scratch building with card filled in the empty wheel wells and the radar direction finders both sides of the nose were made from soldered copper wire. These were fitted last to avoid knocking them off before the model was finished.

Eduard's window mask set CX018 saved a lot of time and is worth the money. The engine cowls were first sprayed with SMS Aluminium acrylic lacquer as a few chips were added later around the access panels. A few more scratches were added later with AK weathering pencils.

Various Mr Hobby Aqueous 52, 78, 80, and 304 Olive Drab acrylics did the upper surfaces and Tamiya XF-19 Sky Grey was the closest match for Neutral Grey keeping in mind the weathering processes followed were going to darken the finish. At each stage a soft cloth was used to lightly buff the paint after it had thoroughly dried to remove any overspray and trapped dust.

Decals were applied with the aid of Tamiya decal adhesive and Mr Softer was used to settle the decals down into any panel lines they had covered. After these were sealed with a clear coat of floor polish, weathering started with Tamiya's dark brown accent colour along all the panel lines; various oils and acrylics created all the stains and streaks. Humbrol Matt Clear flattened the finish nicely as did a final buff with that soft cloth.

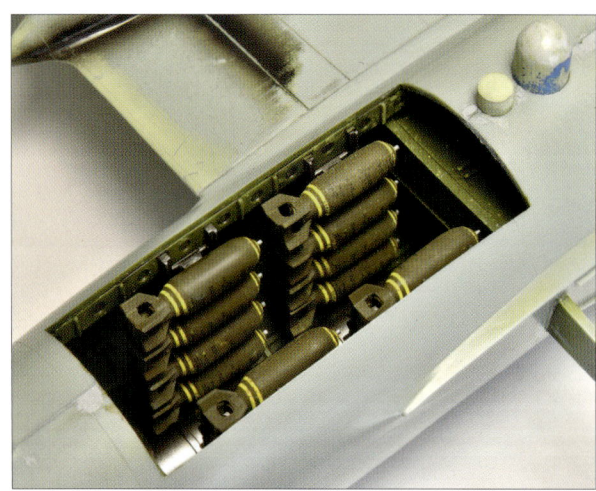

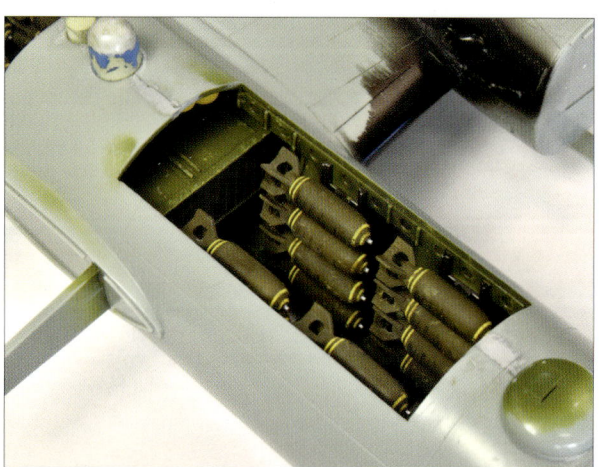
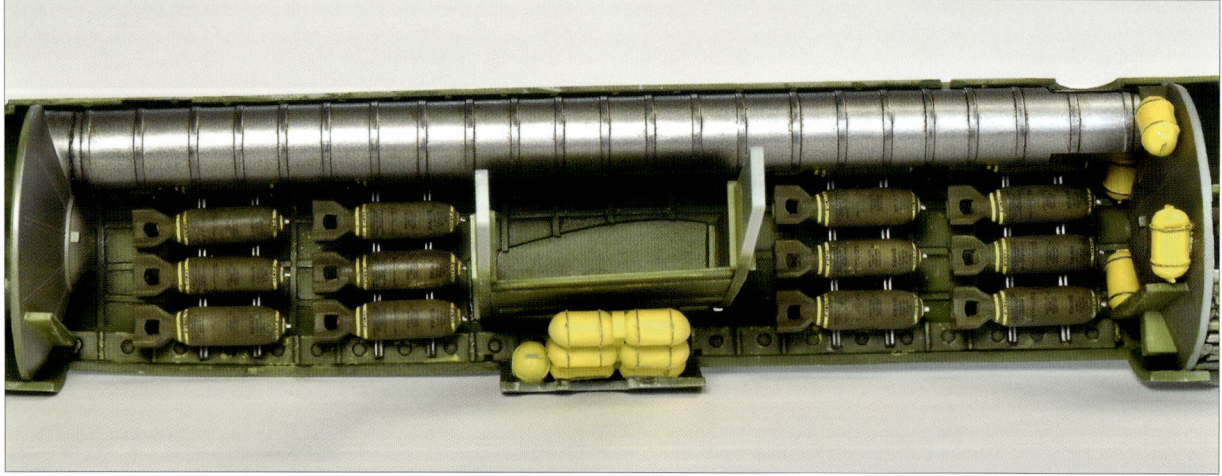
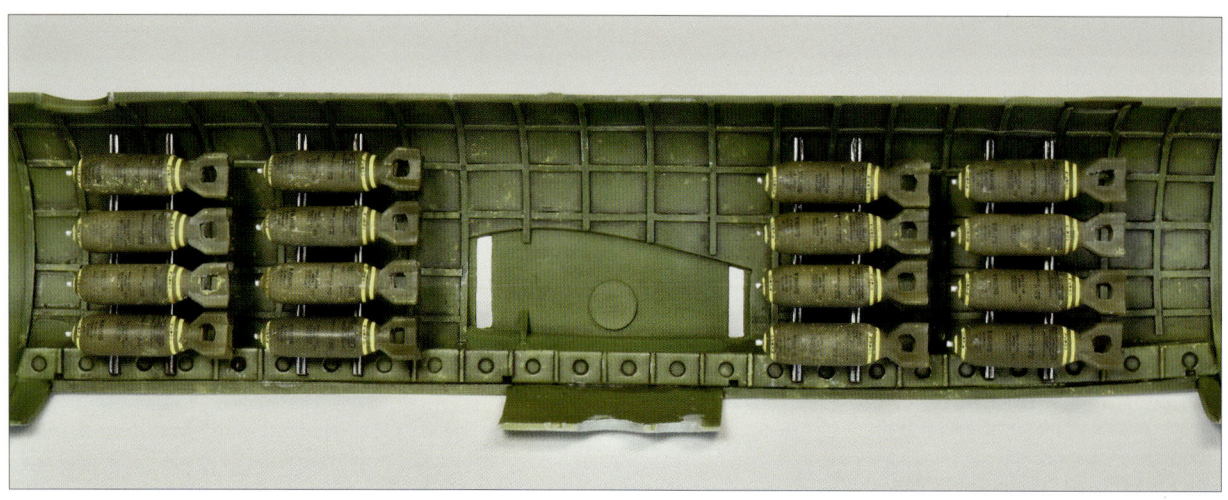

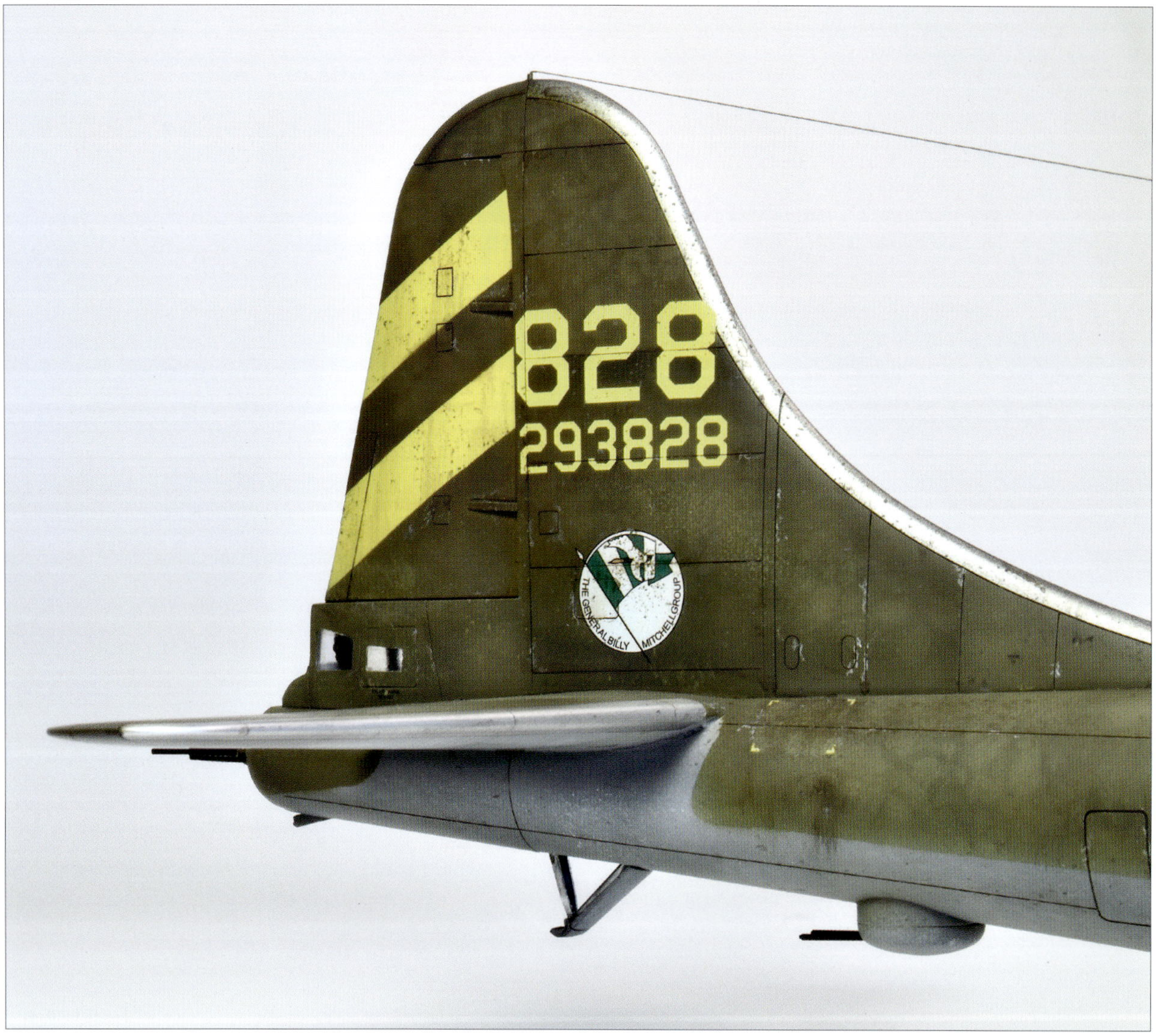
828
293828
THE GENERAL BILLY MITCHELL GROUP

828
293828
THE GENERAL BILLY MITCHELL GROUP

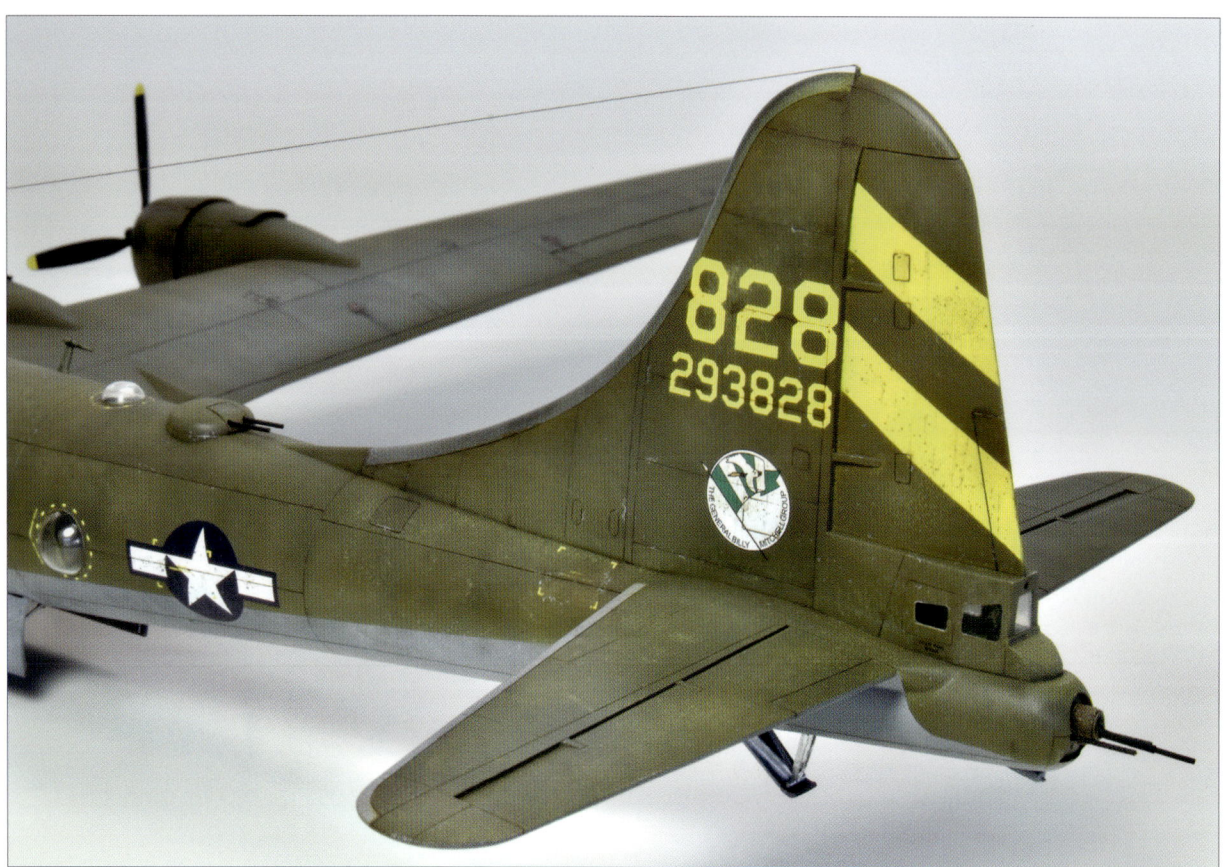

Modelling the Boeing B-29 83

828
U.S. ARMY AIR FORCES

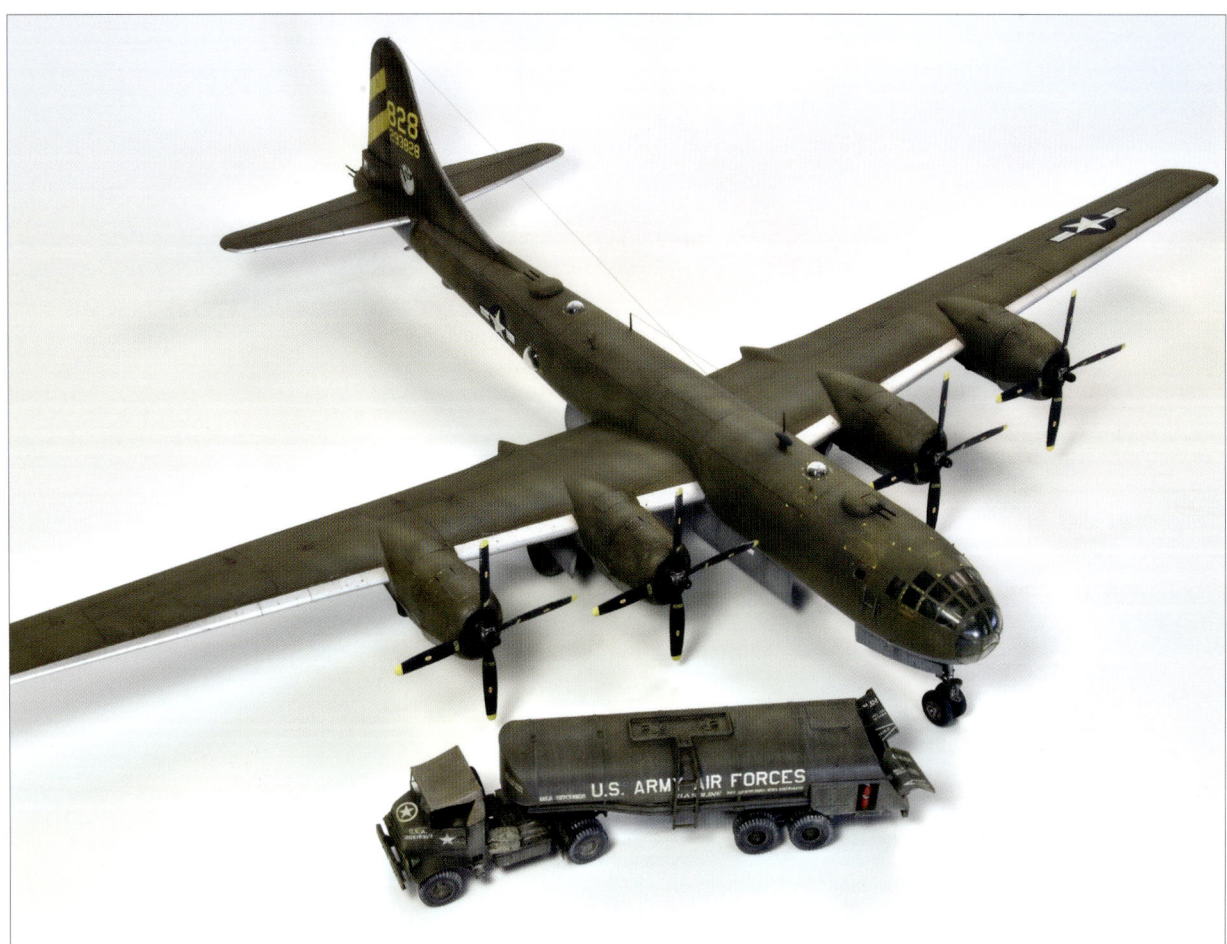

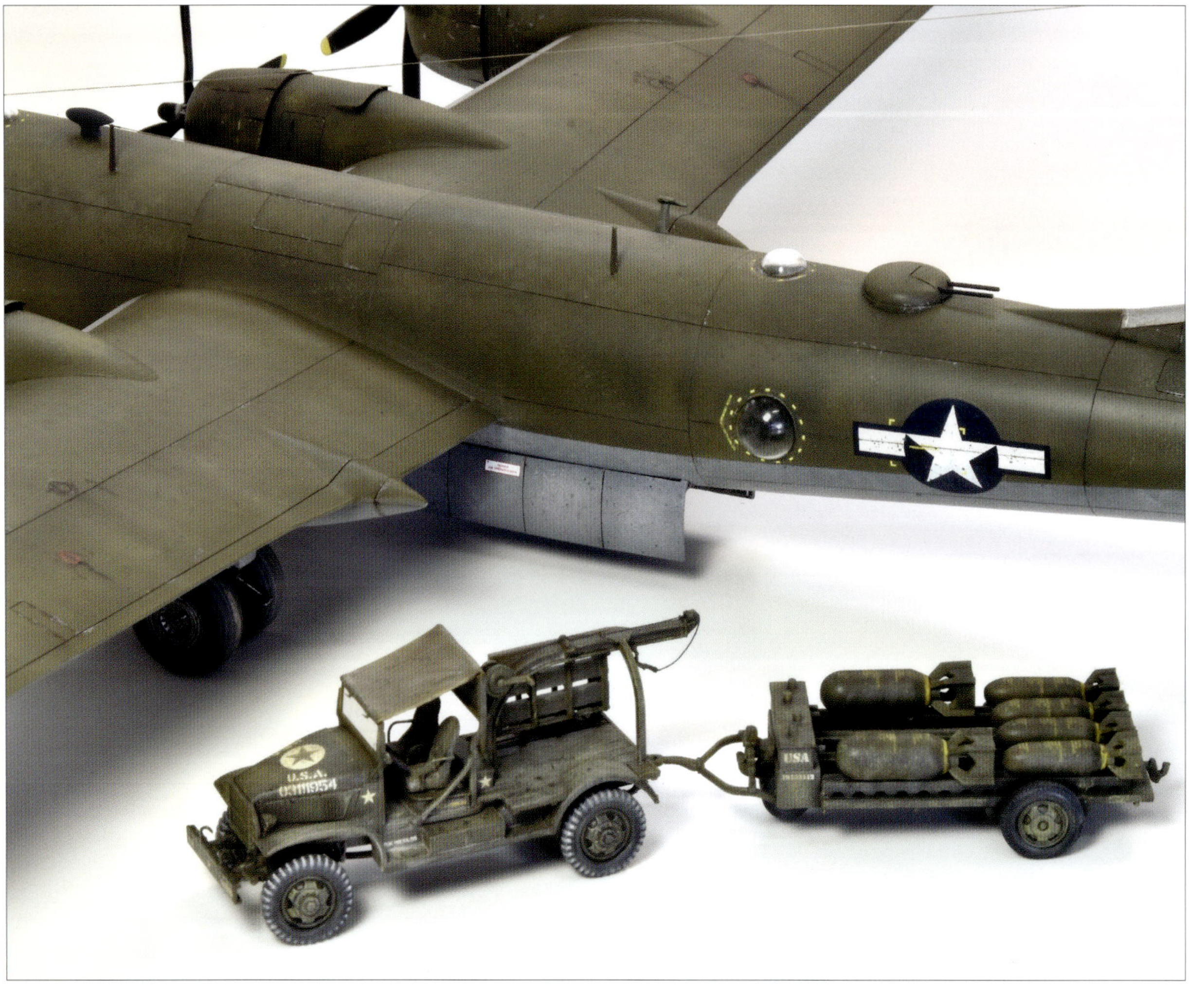
U.S.A.
USA

Boeing Washington B.1 WW354, Royal Australian Air Force
Academy 1/72 B-29
Modelled by Brian Richardson

WW354 was built from the 1/72 Academy 'Enola Gay'/'Bockscar' kit as it contains all the necessary parts with both cuffed and un-cuffed props and the gun turret blanks. Academy's kit is a straight-forward, basic build with a few fit issues that need a few refinements. Reference photos show the Astro dome kit part i151 was moved forward to where the gun turret was removed; an easy fix is to drill out the turret blank and fill in the now-unused hole in the fuselage with card. Clear parts i164 and 165 blank off the waist blisters. Photos show the window/port hole forward of centre. A disc of masking tape was punched out and covered these for painting later.

The cockpit was detailed with Eduard ED72204 photoetch and the wheel wells with Metallic Details MD7204 which includes replacement resin engines and exhausts. The engine cooling flaps needed thinning down, this was done with a scalpel scraping away excess plastic. The Eduard set has individual photoetch flaps that allows them to be shown open or closed. Here the easier thinned plastic look has been selected.

Extra packing with scrap styrene card behind the engines gave the nacelles more support when fitted to the wings and allowed for the slight gap to show as well. The engine inspection covers were given a few screws with Trumpeter's riveting tool.

Relying on photo references, the propellor blades were swapped over by drilling and pinning the cuffed blades and fitting them to the more accurate and detailed hubs from the other set. Reference photos show that the rear gun site and twin Browning .50's were still fitted in the tail while in Australia. The guns were removed sometime before the aircraft was sold off for scrap. A couple of barrels were borrowed from a Master B-17 set and are a big improvement and a lot stronger than the kit parts.

The model has a weathered natural metal finish as WW354 would have appeared in RAF service prior to being flown to Australia. At that time most RAAF aircraft in service were painted flat aluminium. After priming with Tamiya X-1 Gloss Black various metallics from the Alclad II and SMS acrylic lacquer range were used. A clear coat of SMS super clear was applied before and after the decals, and a panel-line wash of ground black pastel chalk mixed with water and a drop of dish washing liquid was applied.

A water-based wash, after it has dried, is much safer to remove with a water-dampened tissue than an oil-based product as these metallic paints can be quite sensitive to oils and even methylated spirit can cause damage.

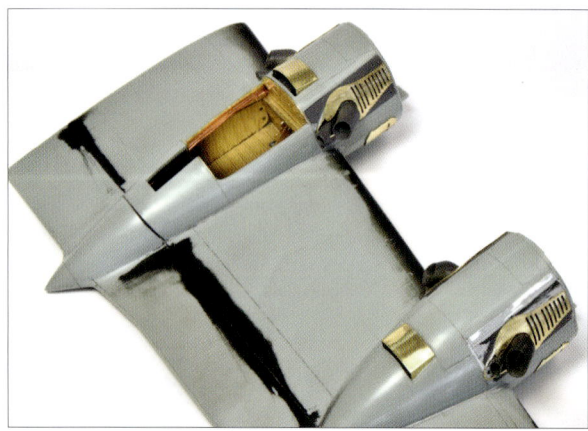
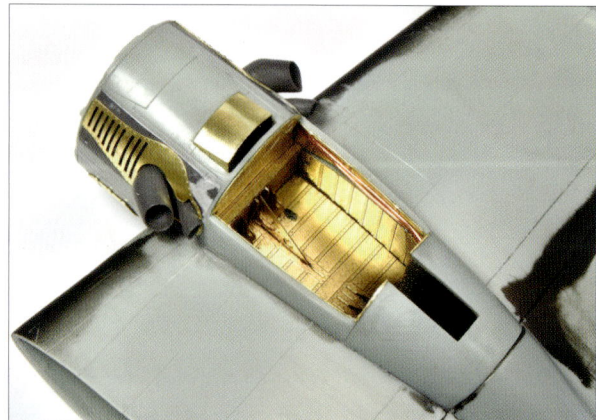

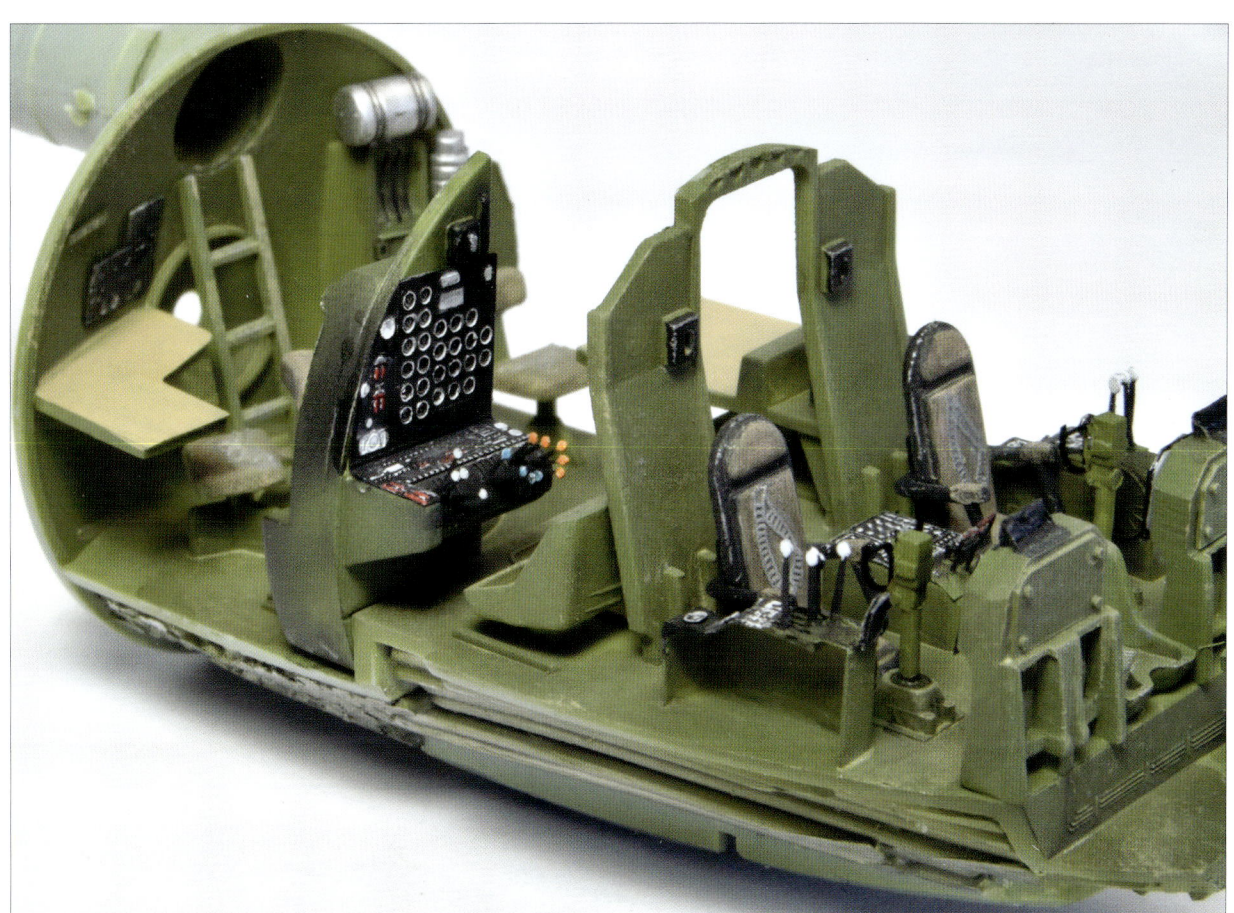

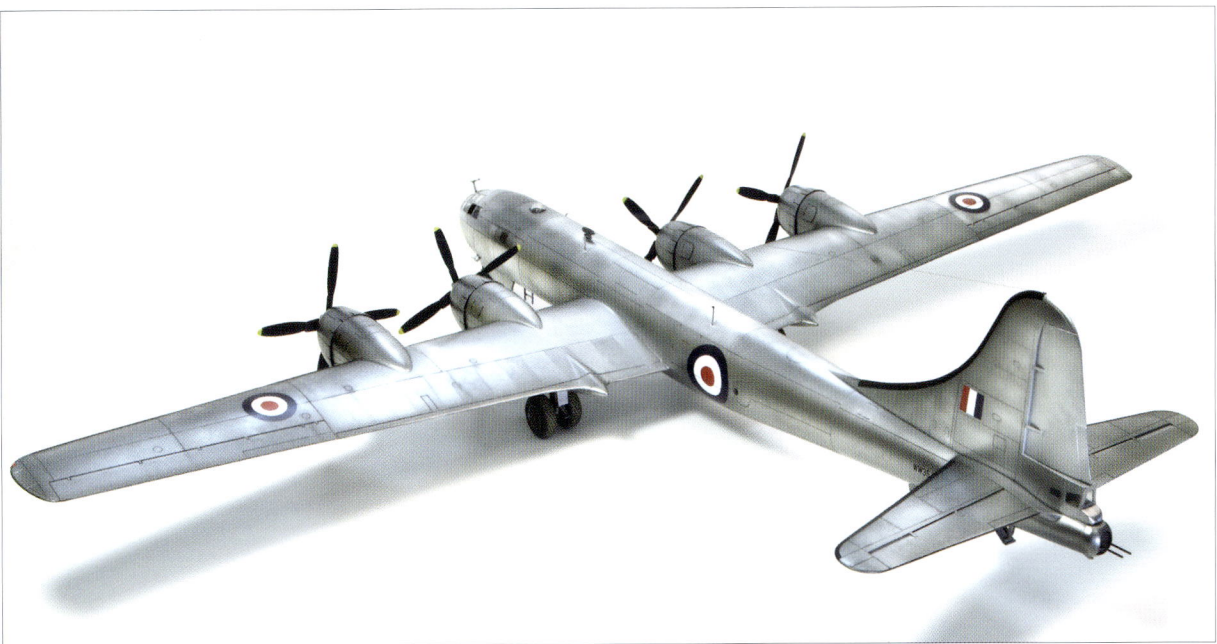

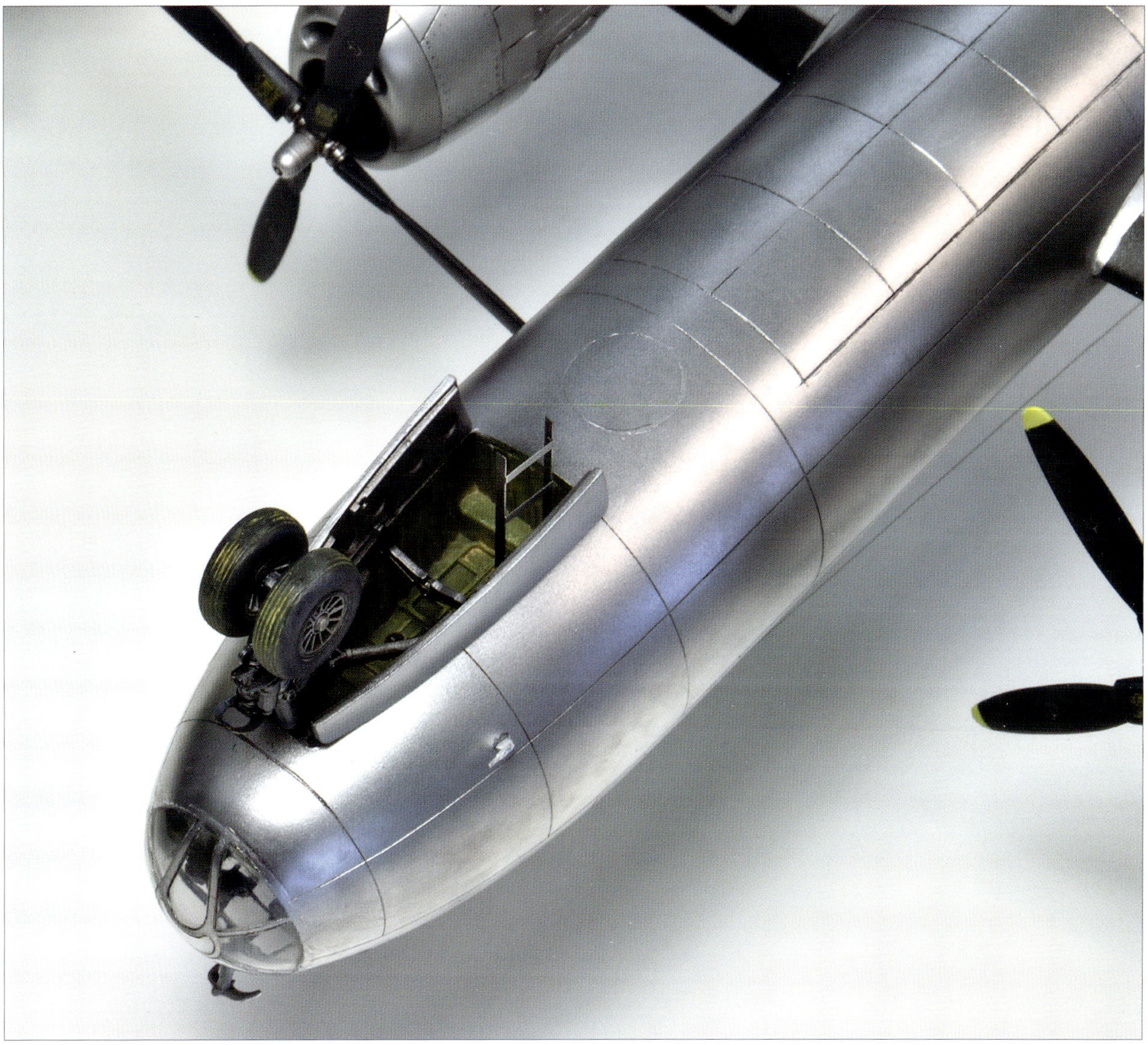